An Introduction to Herbal Teas and Natural Remedies

Discover 100+ Herbal Tea Infusion Recipes for Holistic Healing and Greater Well Being

The Green Glow

Contents

Freebies For Our Supporters!

We've got a nice beginner recipe book for all of you herbal newbies out there. Just scan the code below to claim yours!

I want my freebie!

Join Our Budding Community!

We have a brand new community and we want **YOU** to help us grow! Are you willing to be one of the first seeds in our Facebook garden? Do you have any questions? Do you want share your herbal world with us and our glowing community? If you answered yes to any of these then, well, what are you waiting for? Just scan the code to join our community!

Join the Facebook group: Herbs, Heart, and Healing

Introduction

"Tea is the elixir of life."

— Lao Tzu

Prior to sitting down to write the first word on my new book about tea, naturally I made a cup of tea. Grounding myself with the familiar ritual of making a cup of tea was exactly what I needed when starting the big venture of a book on a topic I feel so passionate about. Tea is an intrinsic part of my life, and many comforting brews accompanied the words, recipes, and topics you are about to encounter.

Food and drink have the unique ability to transport us back in time to another moment when we had the opportunity to enjoy them, even if it wasn't the first time they became part of our lives. Hibiscus tea takes me back to the Sunday morning breakfast in my grandparents' kitchen. Black tea transports me to sitting on my friend's couch. Artichoke tea reminds me of the always too-ambitious holiday dinner. Green tea with jasmine fills me with the excitement of something new. Tea is a charming bookmark in the anthology of our life experiences that enthralls us with its aroma and transports us to different places and times—all from the comfort of our armchairs.

Ordinarily, we'd only call *tea* an infusion of the *Camellia sinensis* plant. You might be more familiar with it when it's called white, green, oolong, or black tea. White tea is made out of the Camellia leaves that have been picked right after the buds are fully open. Green tea is made out of Camellia leaves that haven't been fermented, and it's the reason why it keeps the color of its leaves even after drying. Oolong tea is made out of leaves that are only partially fermented, which gives the brew its green-black color. Black tea, also known as red tea in some parts of the world, is made from fermented tea leaves.

The hot water infusion of any other herb, spice, rhizome, bark, root, fruit, or flower other than *Camellia sinensis* is typically called a *tisane*. Some people might get stuck in separating true teas from tisanes, and leaf infusions from flower infusions. However, to avoid long-winded explanations throughout the book, I will conventionally refer to all *Camellia sinensis* and tisanes as simply *teas*.

When past generations were looking to alleviate pain or heal illness, they looked to a solution in the natural world around them. Whether that solution cropped up as a *Camellia sinensis* tea, or as tisane, it didn't really matter much. What mattered was its beneficial effect and taste. However, it should be noted that teas are naturally caffeinated, whereas tisanes are naturally caffeine-free.

As far as we know, Ancient Egyptians and Chinese civilizations were the first to experiment with herbal teas to treat health issues. Certain dried peppermint leaves have even made their way into Egyptian pyramids—that's how deeply revered they were in Egyptian life and beyond. Throughout history, tea has been as much of a necessity for maintaining health as it has been a pleasure.

A culture whose references to tea go back even further than the Egyptians is the ancient Chinese civilization. According to folklore, the first tea was created in 2737 B.C.E. when a Camellia blossom made its way into Emperor Shen Nung's boiled drinking water. What a strategic blossom that one was! However, we might just have to thank it for all the medicinal qualities we later discovered teas to possess.

For a long time, tea was known for its great digestive benefits, which is why Chinese civilizations have been consuming it regularly after meals. Teas were simply practical beverages that aided health. However, that changed in the eighth century when Buddhist monk named Lu Yu wrote *The Classic of Tea* and elevated tea to a beverage worthy of celebrations and accompanying moments of personal significance. This is when tea started growing in popularity and became more than a health elixir.

On the topic of support for health and wellness, here are a few reasons why I encourage you to step into the magical world of teas:

- Supporting digestion
- Encouraging detoxification
- Boosting immunity
- Regulating the nervous system to improve relaxation
- Natural sleep support
- Support for healthy skin, hair, and nails
- Improve focus and cognition
- Suppress sugar cravings and control appetite
- If you resonate with any of the areas above, I have a great variety of teas and herb combinations for you.

Moreover, if you want to get even deeper into the vibrant realm teas and employ them to aid men's or women's health challenges, as well as hair and skin issues, I've got you covered. I bet you didn't know that teas can be highly effective at aiding recovery and encouraging physical resilience. Even our energy and focus can be enhanced with the help of teas, as well as our protection against seasonal allergies.

All in all, teas have a holistic effect on our mind and body, helping us in more ways than one. Teas help us not only in functioning optimally, but also to live our lives to the fullest.

Chapter 1

Origins and Traditions

W hen you think about a cup of tea, what imagery pops up in your mind? Does your mind take you to the afternoon tea culture in the United Kingdom, an elaborate, neat Japanese tea ceremony, or does it take you to getting cozy with a book and a great cup of tea on a chilly afternoon? Tea is versatile for many different situations. Tea can be the perfect companion to the most formal event, but it can just as well be an informal, personal ritual you have in the comfort and privacy of your home.

Modern Evolution of Tea Culture

The origin of tea is shrouded in legend, and it is difficult to pinpoint the actual provenance place, but it has slowly become an undeniably monumental industry. Whether it emerged as a preferred beverage in China, Tibet, or North India is still unclear. What is certain is that during the Chinese Tang dynasty (618–907), tea grew in popularity so much that it warranted a government-imposed tax and the aforementioned bestseller written by Lu Yu. The following centuries only increased the fashionableness of tea in East Asia with it becoming a popular muse in poetry and the arts.

In the 9th century, tea made its way to Japan by means of another Buddhist monk, Saichō. After studying in China, he collected some tea seeds. Being endowed with a green thumb, Saichō started growing tea at his monastery and was quickly accompanied by his fellow monks. Considering that it was only monasteries that grew tea plants in Japan, it was only in the 13th century that its popularity started blossoming. Unlike the Chinese, who infused their leaves whole, the Japanese preferred grinding the delicate leaves into a powder that is still of the essence on any hip cafe's menu —matcha.

The rest of the world soon started trading with East Asia and an entirely new world of ideas, foods, customs, beverages, philosophies, and possibilities opened up. Tea followed suit and became a staple in many households all over the world. Europe was quite late to the game, with tea only being considered a worthy trading good when the Dutch East India Company popularized it in the 17th century. Even so, it was a pleasure made available exclusively to the aristocracy and royalty at first. The British, in particular, were reluctant to forego coffee for the milder tea. Soon, the British understood tea's trading potential and built something akin to a tea monopoly despite the avid competition they faced and the challenges posed by tea-smuggling operations that were active on the same territory.

Being the romantic era of exploration, adventure, and piracy, it's no surprise that the British even sent an undercover botanist, Robert Fortune, to China to learn everything about tea varieties and planting in the hopes of becoming less dependent on the Chinese growers. After successful tea plantings in two regions in India that might sound familiar now due to the tea varieties with the same name, Assam and Darjeeling, the British have finally managed to move their tea growing outside of China. After this, the sky was-limit for the British Empire in the tea industry.

Tea made its way to America at the same time and in a similar manner to how it reached Britain—in the 17th century by the Dutch. Dominance over the territory quickly changed hands and was now in British possession. Supported by government policies that favored British tea traders and excluded colonial merchants, the British managed to build a tea trading empire on the East Coast of North America. The British monopoly on tea later turned out to be a vulnerable house of cards, as the Boston Tea Party occurred. While protesting the high taxes, colonists dressed up as Native Americans, boarded British East India Company ships, and threw the entire tea supply overboard.

The closer we get in time to the present day, the more tea grows in popularity and availability. We can trace the origins of iced tea back to 1904 in St. Louis, Missouri. Around this same time, the first patent for a tea bag was invented. Opening our cupboards today and looking at the variety of tea available—whether loose leaves, powder, or tea bags—hopefully this history lesson helps you appreciate the long journey tea has been on to make tea time as timeless as its aroma.

Tips: Adapting Global Traditions Into Daily Rituals

Nowadays, a tea party might not look like it once did, with opulent garments and polite conversation, but it might become a tea party for one—or more—in comfortable pajamas with a good movie or book. What was a social event in the past can easily become a self-care party in the present. Let's allow tea to remind us that we need a great balance between work, social life, and alone time to function at our most harmonious best. Why not enjoy a delicious cup of tea in the tranquility of our homes, regardless if we're accompanied or not?

The Green Glow

If you're a fellow tea aficionado, you will find creative ways to integrate tea into your daily rituals. In the comfort of our homes, no etiquette needs to be followed. At home, there is no compulsion to brew and serve our tea a certain way. We make the rules and enjoy tea to our liking. However, to ensure we get the most out of it, there are a few suggestions regarding water temperature, brewing times, and preserving our tea that we'll get into more in-depth next.

Chapter 2

Basic Principles

Attending a specialized tea house is certainly an unforgettable treat and one that we should all experience at least once. However, on a more frequent basis, most of us are not consuming tea in luxurious tea houses but rather in the comfort of home. There's something so comforting about holding a hot cup of tea in your hands and inhaling the promise of a mind-altering aroma.

The Diverse Palette of Herbal Flavors and Aromas

When the world of tea unravels its mysteries before our eyes—or should I say taste buds—it truly feels like a new world of aromas has materialized. Some aromas might be familiar to us from the corresponding foods, but many will take us down a path of more subtle and intricate aromas. Certain flavors will be bold and demand all of our palate's attention, while others will be more shy and will wait to be discovered by those interested in digging deeper. While we already covered the typical white, green, oolong, and black teas made by brewing *Camellia sinensis* leaves, this time we'll journey a bit farther into herbal teas made from spices, dried fruits, flowers, and herbs. All of these teas have incontestable health benefits, but with difficulty on my part, I will hold off on that information until the next chapters where I'll expand on this facet of teas.

Chamomile tea is made by brewing chamomile flowers, which are tiny with a daisy-like appearance. Chamomile is an herb from the Asteraceae family alongside—not surprisingly—daisies, sunflowers, and marigolds. The two varieties used for making tea are the Roman one, *Chamaemelum nobile*, and the German variety, *Matricaria recutita*. Due to a high concentration of chemicals named flavonoids, chamomile tea has many health benefits. Chamomile tea can ameliorate menstrual syndromes, calm inflammation, and improve sleep quality. When it comes to taste, chamomile tea has a mild aroma with mellow notes of apple and honey-like sweetness.

Peppermint tea is exactly what it sounds like—refreshing, cooling, minty, and delicious. The peppermint plant *Mentha x piperita* is a cross between spearmint and water mint.

Out of all the teas, this is probably the one most people are familiar with because the herb is also used to flavor breath mints, candy, and a lot of other foods. On top of peppermint tea being a great beverage to help cool off in the hottest months, it also has anti-inflammatory, antiviral, and antibacterial properties. Peppermint oil, which is more concentrated than peppermint tea, has proven to be quite eff ective in ameliorating irritable bowel syndrome (IBS) symptoms.

Ginger tea, with its tangy taste, has proven to be excellent at relieving nausea, regardless if it is digestion-related, pregnancy-related, or cancer treatment-related. As the "officinale" in its scientific name suggests—*Zingiber officinale*—ginger has been used as medicine for thousands of years to treat ailments such as colds, nausea, and even arthritis by boiling the peeled root in water or

- What should be the water-to-tea ratio?
- Can I boil tap water?

If you are about to use loose-leaf to make your herbal tea, it is important that you focus on the water-to-tea ratio. For every 6–8 ounces of water, you can roughly add 1–2 teaspoons (because you are making tea) of loose leaves, depending upon how strong you like it. Generally, the teapot or kettle can hold around 24 ounces of water. This means that you can add about 5 teaspoons of loose-leaf tea to get a perfect flavor.

Make sure that you are using distilled water to make your tea. Distilled water is best because it is free from any impurities and chemicals. Before adding the tea, wait till the temperature of water is around 100° C from boiling.

Add Herbs

Now, time for your favorite herbs to go in. The herbs will be responsible for bringing the flavor you are looking for, so make sure you are adding the just right amount.

If you are using a ready-made blend, read the package instructions to find out the mentioned brewing time. The instructions are written by professionals, so following those will give you a perfect flavor.

Boil for Two Minutes

Once you have added the herbs to the water, bring the mixture to a boil for 1-2 minutes. Do not add herbs to cold water, as it will result in a condensed and bitter brew instead of a fresh herbal tea.

Steep for Five Minutes

When done boiling, remove the kettle from heat. Let your mixture rest for approximately five minutes. Meanwhile, cover the kettle or pot with a lid so that the steam remains inside.

Strain Your Herbal Tea

With the help of a strainer, strain the tea into a cup. You can also squeeze a lemon or add honey into your tea, but this is totally optional.

And you're done. You can now enjoy your tea.

Storage and Freshness: Maintaining Potency

No one wants their tea to taste stale, right? To get the full benefits of each herb every time, storing your tea in the right way will help you.

Here are some factors that affect the shelf life of your tea directly:

- The type of your tea matters. There are many different types of herbal teas available. Each of them carries unique characteristics and shelf life.
- The storage conditions also come into play. If the temperature, exposure to air, and humidity are ideal, the shelf life of tea increases.
- The packaging type of your tea also affects the shelf life. If teabags or loose leaves are in an airtight container, they tend to last longer.
- Tea comes in two main forms, including tea bags and loose leaves. Tea bags typically have a shorter shelf life than loose leaves.

Taking these factors into account, if you have stored your herbal tea properly, it can retain maximum flavor for 1–2 years.

How to Store Your Herbal Tea

Pick a Good Storage Container

Your storage container can keep your tea fresh for a prolonged period. Therefore, there is no harm in investing in an airtight container. Usually, airtight containers are made up of glass, but you can also opt for other non-reactive materials. As a result, your tea will stay fresh. Other examples of non-reactive materials include stainless steel or ceramic containers.

Brown paper bags also work well to store tea, as they do not increase moisture or leave an odor.

Do not opt for a plastic container. Plastic is known for absorbing unwanted odors.

Keep Away From Direct Sunlight

Exposure to sunlight can affect the quality of tea, making it lose its flavor and aroma. You can place your container in a cool, dark place and away from direct sunlight. If not, use an opaque container that will shield your tea from the direct sunlight.

Be Cautious of the Heat

If the temperature around your tea is constantly fluctuating, it can cause the leaves to deteriorate. You must keep the storage away from stoves or ovens.

When to Worry

Here are some indicators that can tell if your tea has expired:

- Expired leaves can cause a **foul smell**. If not foul, you will not be able to smell anything at all, and it represents that the tea is no longer potent.

- With time, tea leaves can start to **taste bitter** or flat. This means that the leaves have lost their natural oils and it is time for you to replace them.
- **Color change** is also associated with your tea going bad. Observe closely to see if your tea bags or leaves have changed in color.

Tips: Tools of the Trade—Essential Tea Paraphernalia

If you are a tea lover, there is a list of essentials to keep at hand. Some of the short-listed tools include teapots, tea strainers or infusers, tea cups, tea thermometers, tea scoops or spoons, and tea storage. The list can go on, but these are the basic tools you will need to brew yourself a good cup of tea.

Teapot

Teapots come in different shapes and sizes. However, when buying one, consider the material it is made of, as it can impact the flavor of your tea. Many people prefer using a teapot made up of ceramic or porcelain. Both of these materials are best known for not absorbing any flavor.

Tea Infusers of Strainers

Tea infusers or strainers are best for environmentally conscious people. With them, you can have a reusable option every time, instead of using disposable tea bags for your tea. These are essential to strain your tea, allowing loose leaves to release their full flavor as you pour.

Teacups

Everyone has a personal favorite teacup. You can choose your teacup based on your aesthetic preferences and tea-drinking style. There are so many designs and sizes to choose from on the market.

and water retention, potentially supporting weight-loss efforts when combined with a healthy diet and lifestyle.

- A detoxed body is better equipped to support a robust immune system. The immune system can function more efficiently, helping the body defend against infections and illnesses.
- Detoxification may also have cognitive benefits, enhancing mental clarity and improving concentration.
- Detoxification can contribute to the reduction of inflammation in the body.
- Supporting hormonal balance is potential benefit of detoxification.

Now that you have read all of that, you're probably wanting to know how you can go about cleansing your precious machine, aka your body. Well, now that we're friends, I'll let you in on a little secret: Herbal teas can do all of that and much more. They support the body's natural detox processes. Certain herbs possess properties that enhance liver function, promote kidney health, and provide antioxidant support.

For instance, dandelion and milk thistle are known to support liver detoxification, while nettle and parsley contribute to kidney health. Incorporating herbal teas into your daily routine not only provides hydration but also offers a flavorful and accessible means to fortify the body's natural detox mechanisms, promoting overall health and vitality.

Herbs Renowned for Aiding Digestion and Promoting Detox

Nature has given you tons of herbs that help you attain optimal digestive health and promote detoxification. These herbs not only enhance the digestive process but also contribute to the body's natural detox mechanisms. Incorporating these herbs into your daily routine is an easy way to improve your mental and physical health.

Peppermint tea is known for its ability to alleviate indigestion and soothe an upset stomach. It relaxes the muscles of the gastrointestinal tract, promoting the flow of bile for effective digestion. The antimicrobial properties of peppermint aid in cleansing the digestive system by helping to expel unwanted bacteria. It can also assist in reducing bloating and gas, contributing to a comfortable digestion.

Ginger tea stimulates saliva production and suppresses gastric contractions as food and fluids move through the GI tract. It is particularly effective against nausea and can enhance nutrient absorption. Ginger's antioxidant properties contribute to detoxification by neutralizing harmful free radicals. It also supports liver function, a key player in the body's detox processes.

Turmeric tea contains curcumin, which helps stimulate bile production, aiding in the breakdown of fats. It also has anti-inflammatory properties that can reduce digestive discomfort. Curcumin supports liver detoxification pathways, assisting in the removal of toxins. Its antioxidant properties further contribute to overall cellular health.

Fennel tea has carminative properties, reducing gas and bloating. It can also relax the intestines, easing digestive spasms and promoting smoother digestion. Fennel's diuretic properties aid in the elimination of toxins through urine, supporting kidney function. Its fiber content also helps with regular bowel movements.

Dandelion tea stimulates digestion by balancing the natural and beneficial bacteria in the intestines. It can relieve constipation and improve nutrient absorption. Dandelion acts as a diuretic,

Cook Time: 15 minutes

Ingredients

- ½ teaspoon dried dandelion root pieces
- ½ teaspoon dried burdock root pieces
- 1 teaspoon dried nettle leaves
- 1 cup water

Directions

1. Simmer dandelion root, burdock root, and nettle leaves in freshly boiled water for 15 minutes.
2. Strain and sip throughout the day for a deep detox experience.

Cinnamon Spice Tea

Time: 10 minutes

Serving Time: Evenings

Prep Time: 5 minutes

Cook Time: 5 minutes

Ingredients

- 3 cinnamon sticks
- 5 cardamom pods
- 1 clove
- 1 cup water

Directions

1. Steep cinnamon sticks, cardamom pods, and clove in freshly boiled water for a soothing aroma.

2. Sip during chilly evenings for a calming experience.

Chamomile Tea

Time: 12 minutes

Serving Time: Anytime

Prep Time: 5 minutes

Cook Time: 7 minutes

Ingredients

- 1 teaspoon chamomile flowers
- 1/4th teaspoon dried lavender buds
- 1 cup water

Directions

1. Steep chamomile flowers and lavender buds in hot water for 5–7 minutes.

Licorice Lavender Blend

Time: 15 minutes

Serving Time: Anytime

Prep Time: 5 minutes

Cook Time: 10 minutes

Ingredients

- ½ teaspoon dried licorice root pieces
- 1/4th teaspoon dried lavender buds
- 1 cup water

roasted veggies, or grain bowls. It also offers anti-inflammatory benefits for a healthy meal.

- Citrus tea is ideal for cleansing your palate after rich meals. Zesty citrus notes cut through richness, providing a refreshing finish.
- Fennel tea is aromatic and slightly sweet. This tea enhances Mediterranean flavors, making it a brilliant match for grilled fish or roasted lamb.
- Dandelion detox tea works well with whole foods, like grains, lean proteins, and veggies, for a detoxifying meal.
- Cinnamon spice tea is comforting and aromatic. Start your day with it, pairing it with oatmeal, toast, or yogurt for a cozy breakfast.
- Chamomile calm tea has soothing properties, making it perfect for light snacks. For a calming experience, enjoy it with crackers, cheese, or fresh fruit.
- Peppermint bliss tea is a refreshing choice to conclude your meal. Pair with dark chocolate or fruit sorbet for a satisfying finish.
- Licorice lavender tea has sweet and floral notes, making it delightful with lavender-infused desserts.
- Cumin comfort tea pairs well with spiced dishes incorporating cumin, coriander, and fennel for a satisfying meal.

Chapter 4

Immunity Boost and Stress Relief

Ⅰn the hectic era of modern life, where deadlines dance with daily chores and stress lurks in the shadows of our every move, tea has become more than just a beverage to its lovers. Living a stressful life could potentially lead you into a spiral of unhealthy habits and with that, could lead to a weaker immune system. Tea can help can you on the straight and narrow in a bit of a "two birds one stone" type of way.

First and foremost, let's talk immunity—a shield that stands guard against the unseen invaders threatening your well-being. When it comes to enhancing your body's natural defense mechanisms, herbal teas have emerged as unsung heroes in this quest for robust health.

On the other hand, stress relief also emerges as a recurrent theme in the labyrinth of herbal teas. Often, tea acts as a soothing balm for the turbulence of daily life. To give you a more holistic view of the health benefits of herbal teas, this chapter unfolds the botanical wonderland of a variety of herbs for you. So, let's uncover the captivating tales of herbs together and learn new ways to treat your taste buds while boosting your immunity below!

Understanding the Immune System

Herbal teas, with their potent botanical allies, can be instrumental in fortifying your immunity. However, before getting into the complexities of how they boost this vital defense mechanism, it is essential to grasp the basics of the immune system itself.

How Does the Immune System Work?

Your body's defense system works through a multiple-step process with different mechanisms. However, this complex structure of defense can be divided into two main classes of immunity—innate immunity and adaptive immunity.

Innate Immunity

Innate immunity is the natural defense system of your body that you are born with. By nature, innate immunity is a rough and unsophisticated defense mechanism, but it is also a rapid-response team. So, the next time you dodge a cold or shake off a minor infection without breaking a sweat, thank your innate immune system for its no-nonsense, always-on-duty approach!

Adaptive Immunity

On the other hand, adaptive immunity is the type of immunity that develops in response to exposure to pathogens or vaccination. Also known as acquired immunity, it provides immunological memory, enabling a quicker and more robust reaction upon re-exposure to the same pathogen. This system's specificity and memory contribute to long-term protection, offering a sophisticated defense against a wide array of infectious agents, viruses, and bacteria

Herbal Allies Against Stress and Immunity Challenges

The usage of herbs and natural botanicals is no secret when it comes to immunity boosting and stress relieving. This practice has been already used in Indian Ayurvedic medicine and other cultural traditional healing modalities for centuries. Some of the common herbs that help reduce stress and anxiety while boosting your immunity are given below:

Ginger Tea is the most common and most well-known immunity-boosting herb. This underground root has been a staple in traditional medicine for centuries. The active ingredients include gingerol and shogaol compounds.

Turmeric Tea, a golden-hued spice, is another one of the magical secrets used in Indian Ayurvedic medicine. Just like ginger, it boasts potent herbal properties that make it an excellent addition to herbal teas for immune support and stress relief. Curcumin also supports neurotransmitters such as serotonin, potentially enhancing mood.

Echinacea Tea, renowned for its immune-boosting properties, is a stellar addition to herbal teas that double as stress relievers. Echinacea has a long history of medicinal use with Native American tribes. This herb is rich in bioactive compounds, including alkamides, polysaccharides, and flavonoids, which collectively stimulate the immune system.

Paprika Tea may sound unusual, but paprika is one of the richest sources of antioxidants and anti-inflammatory agents. Paprika is a spice made from dried and ground red peppers called *Capsicum annuum*. When combined with other herbal teas, paprika provides excellent taste as well as a health boost.

Peppermint Tea, a powerhouse in herbal teas, is full of immune-supporting and stress-relieving properties. Peppermint's active compound, menthol, has antimicrobial effects. The germ-fighting capabilities of menthol aid in respiratory health and immune function.

Hibiscus Tea, otherwise known as *Hibiscus rosa-sinensis,* is an evergreen shrub that surprisingly belongs to the cotton family. Hibiscus tea high in vitamin C, which is an antioxidant and powerful immune system ally. Hibiscus is delightfully tart, similar to raspberry or cranberry, with a vibrant deep red color.

Lemongrass Tea has a distinct mellow citrus and lightly grassy flavor. Lemongrass grows in stalks and can be difficult to find in your average grocery store or supermarket, however visiting your local Asian market is almost guaranteed to send you home with fresh lemongrass stalks. Two essential oils of lemongrass- citral and citronellal, are very well known for their relaxing aroma.

Chamomile Tea is such an effective stress-reducing tea that it even has a reputation for inducing sleepiness. Additionally, research studies have shown that chamomile tea can reduce the symptoms of generalized anxiety disorder. Best of all, chamomile tea has a lightly floral taste that agrees with the tastebuds of the vast majority of people.

Tulsi Tea, otherwise known as holy basil, is an Indian Ayurvedic herb. As the name suggests, tulsi is a variety of basil. However, this herb does not belong in your caprese salad like Italian basil. Tulsi is an adaptogenic herb, meaning it helps the mind and body become more resilient to stressors.

Lavender Tea features beautiful purple lavender buds, which grow in full sun areas. Lavender aromatherapy has been well-studied to reduce stress and anxiety. In fact, a clinical lavender oil has been developed called Silexan which can be taken orally and is well-researched for calming anxiety.

11 Recipes: Blends for Bolstering Immunity and Reducing Stress

Getting out of bed to brew yourself a cup of tea can be too much at times, especially when you are feeling low and drained. So, to help you kick out that lazy bug and ease your procrastination process, we have come up with easy tea blends for you. These mixes will not only recharge your draining energy but also kick-start your immunity.

Haldi Mix

Time: 10 minutes

Serving Time: Anytime

Prep Time: 5 minutes

Cook Time: 10 minutes

Ingredients

- a pinch of haldi powder or a couple of fresh turmeric slices
- a couple of ginger slices
- pinch of black pepper
- honey and lime juice (optional for taste)
- 1 cup water

Directions

1. Take a pot of boiling water and add your ginger slices, a little bit of haldi powder or fresh turmeric slices, and a pinch of pepper.

2. Cover the pot and let it sit for about 10 minutes.
3. Strain your magical concoction and add lime juice or honey as per your liking to give a taste enhancement. And… it's ready!

Peppermint Delight

Time: 2 minutes

Serving Time: Anytime

Prep Time: 2 minutes

Cook Time: 2 minutes

Ingredients

- handful of fresh peppermint leaves
- honey and lime juice (optional for taste)
- 1 cup of water

Directions

1. Boil your water and add freshly picked peppermint leaves to it.
2. Let it brew for 2 minutes.
3. Take it off the flame. Add honey and lime as per your taste and it's ready.

Hibiscus Tea Mix

Time: 10–15 minutes

Serving Time: Anytime

Prep Time: 5 minutes

Cook Time: 10 minutes

The Green Glow

Ingredients

- 1.5 teaspoons dried hibiscus petals
- 1 cup water
- sweetener (any, optional, to taste)

Directions

1. Bring the water to a boil in a saucepan or kettle.
2. Add the dried hibiscus petals to the boiling water.
3. Let it simmer for about 10–15 minutes on low heat.
4. Turn off the heat and let the tea steep for another 5 minutes.
5. Strain the tea and add a sweetener such as honey or sugar of your choice to taste, stirring until dissolved.
6. Let the tea cool down or serve over ice.

Note: You can adjust the amount of hibiscus petals and sweeteners based on your personal preference for strength and sweetness. Enjoy your homemade hibiscus tea!

Lemongrass Honey Blend

Time: 10–15 minutes

Serving Time: Anytime

Prep Time: 5 minutes

Cook Time: 10 minutes

Ingredients

- 1 fresh lemongrass stalks
- 1 cup water
- honey or sweetener of choice (to taste)
- lime or lemon wedges (optional)

- a couple fresh ginger slices (optional)
- mint leaves (optional)

Directions

1. Prepare the lemongrass stalk by removing any dry or woody outer layers to reveal the inner, tender core and cut off the root ends.
2. Bruise the inner core of the lemongrass to release the essential oils. This can be done by hitting the lemongrass with the butt of the knife a few times. Don't pulverize or completely flatten the lemongrass; just lightly bruise it.
3. In a saucepan, bring the water to a boil.
4. Add the prepared lemongrass stalks to the boiling water. Add a few slices of fresh ginger to the pot for an added zing.
5. Reduce the heat and let the mixture simmer for about 10–15 minutes to allow the flavors to infuse.
6. Switch off the flames and strain the tea. Sweeten it with honey or your preferred sweetener, adjusting to your taste.

Chamomile Detox

Time: 15 minutes

Serving Time: Afternoon

Prep Time: 5 minutes

Cook Time: 10 minutes

Ingredients

- 2 tbsp dried chamomile flowers
- 1 cup water
- A lemon wedge

- honey or sweetener of choice (optional, to taste)

Directions

1. Boil the water and add dried chamomile flowers.
2. Cover and let it steep for about 5 minutes.
3. If desired, add a squeeze of lemon juice to enhance the flavor.
4. Strain the tea to remove the chamomile flowers. Add a sweetener of your choice and enjoy.

Tulsi Spice Mix

Tulsi when combined with ginger creates a delightful stress-fighting and immune-supporting tea. This herbal combination is guaranteed to help you dial down stress and fight colds and the flu simultaneously.

Time: 7 minutes

Serving Time: Anytime

Prep Time: 2 minutes

Cook Time: 5 minutes

Ingredients

- a couple slices of fresh ginger
- 1 tbsp dried holy basil (tulsi leaves)
- honey (optional)

Directions

1. Start with the usual step of boiling water and adding all your ingredients
2. Let them infuse for 5 minutes until the water boils.

3. Take off. Add honey and your tulsi mix is ready!

Ginger Tea

Time: 2 minutes

Serving Time: Anytime

Prep Time: 2 minutes

Cook Time: 2 minutes

Ingredients

- 1 cup water
- A few slices of fresh ginger
- add-ons of your choosing (honey, cinnamon, haldi, or lemon juice as per your liking)

Directions

1. Add your water and ginger to a kettle and let it boil for 2 minutes.
2. Strain.
3. Once done, add your additional tasters as per your liking.

Echinacea Immune Enhancer

Time: 12 minutes

Serving Time: Anytime

Prep Time: 2 minutes

Cook Time: 7 minutes

Ingredients

- 2 tsp dried echinacea flowers, leaves, or root

The Green Glow

- 1 cup water
- honey (per taste)
- a lemon wedge

Directions

1. Boil your dried echinacea pieces with the water for 7–10 minutes.
2. Squeeze a lemon wedge into the tea for added flavor.
3. Add honey as per your liking and enjoy!

Spicy Chai

Time: 9 minutes

Serving Time: Preferably morning or afternoon

Prep Time: 3 minutes

Cook Time: 6 minutes

Ingredients

- 1 teaspoon loose masala chai tea blend
- 1 cup milk
- sugar

Directions

1. Add the tea leaves, cardamom, and milk together. Bring the concoction to a simmer.
2. Allow the pot to simmer for a few minutes.
3. Add sugar according to your taste, strain it, and done!

Lavender Brew

Time: 5–7 minutes

Serving Time: Before sleeping

Prep Time: 2 minutes

Cook Time: 5 minutes

Ingredients

- 1–2 tsp dried lavender flowers
- 1 cup water
- honey or sweetener of choice (optional, to taste)

Directions

1. Boil your water in a kettle.
2. Place the dried lavender flowers in a tea infuser or teapot.
3. Pour the boiling water over the lavender in the infuser or teapot. Cover and let it steep for about 5–7 minutes to allow the calming properties and floral flavors to infuse into the tea.
4. Once done, add honey as per your taste and enjoy your tea!

Tips: Crafting a Routine for Better Defense

Developing a strong immune system is not a day's work. Rather, it needs consistency and proper routine to build up. Only then you'll be able to fight off infections and live a healthy, stress-free life. Here are a few tips that can help you do so:

- Start your day with a cup of green tea enriched with antioxidants to boost metabolism and support overall well-being.
- Incorporate an herbal infusion such as echinacea or ginger tea to provide a midday immune system boost.

- Swap sugary beverages with immune-boosting herbal teas throughout the day, keeping your body hydrated while benefiting from herbal properties.
- Sip on a cup of peppermint or chamomile tea for relaxation and stress reduction, as chronic stress can weaken the immune system.
- Enjoy a calming blend such as lavender to promote restful sleep, crucial for a well-functioning immune system.

Incorporating these herbal teas into your daily routine can contribute to a strengthened immune system, supporting your body's natural defense mechanisms.

Chapter 5

Sleep and Relaxation

W ho doesn't love to sleep? The cozy bed at the end of a long day at work is the best thing in the world. But, sometimes, stress gets in the way, and your beauty sleep gets disturbed. However, your days of restless sleep are about to be a thing of the past with the assistance of herbal teas.

In this chapter, we will help you sleep well. We will learn the magic behind sleep cycles and spill the tea on how herbs can be your sleep's BFF, giving you that deep, comfy rest you've been craving. Brace yourself for a lineup of herbal teas that are like lullabies for your relaxation and sleep.

The Science of Sleep and Its Stages

Sleep is a mystery no one has ever been able to solve completely. But thanks to advances in technology and years of research, we have a vague idea of where our mind goes when we sleep. The science of sleep is something that should never be overlooked.

Ever notice how a good night's sleep can make aches and pains vanish? That's your body's repair shop at work during sleep. Sleep releases growth hormones, repairs tissues, and even boosts your immune system, turning you into a self-healing superhero overnight.

These are just some of the benefits of sleep for your body:

- It enhances memory, creativity, and problem-solving skills. Get ready to wake up feeling like Einstein.
- A good night's sleep is the ultimate stress-buster. It helps you handle life's curveballs with a cool head and a dash of optimism.
- It supports a healthy immune system, regulates appetite, and even keeps your heart ticking happily.
- Ever heard of the term "beauty sleep"? It's not just a myth. Sleep helps rejuvenate your skin, preventing wrinkles and giving you that natural glow.

In a nutshell, sleep is the most important part of your day as it is something your body and mind need. It's not just about counting sheep; it's about unlocking the door to a healthier, more vibrant you.

10 Herbs That Induce Relaxation and Deep Sleep

You must be wondering how you can achieve the sleep of your dreams. The kind of sleep that makes you feel refreshed and calm. All you have to do is incorporate some simple habits into your routine. These habits include a good bedtime routine and some herbal teas.

Chamomile Tea, with its delicate daisy-like flowers, isn't just a pretty sight—it's a powerhouse for relaxation. The secret lies in apigenin, a compound that binds to receptors in the brain, promoting a sense of calm. So, as you sip on chamomile tea, envision a serene meadow and let the subtle floral notes carry you into the realm of dreams.

Lavender Tea is the aromatic maestro of tranquility. It's not just about the pleasant scent; lavender harbors linalool, a compound renowned for its anxiety-reducing properties. Inhale the calming aroma—whether from a cup of lavender tea or a few drops of essential oil on your pillow—and feel the day's tensions dissipate.

Valerian Root Tea is the unsung hero in the world of herbal sleep aids. While it may not boast a delightful aroma, its sedative prowess is undeniable. Valerian interacts with GABA receptors in the brain, slowing down nerve impulses and ushering in a profound sense of tranquility.

Passionflower Tea, the graceful dancer of herbal remedies, takes center stage in promoting relaxation. By boosting GABA levels in the brain, it orchestrates a calming symphony that quietens the mind.

Lemon Balm Tea is ideal for stress-busting tranquility, enter lemon balm. Beyond its delightful citrusy scent, this herb contains compounds that effectively calm the nervous system.

Peppermint Tea, usually associated with a burst of freshness, moonlights as a muscle-relaxing maestro. Beyond its invigorating taste, peppermint helps alleviate tension, ensuring your body unwinds as you prepare for sleep.

Ashwagandha Tea is otherwise known as the "Indian ginseng,". Ashwagandha steps into the herbal spotlight as your adaptogenic ally for relaxation. By lowering cortisol levels, it helps the body manage stress effectively.

Ginger Tea, renowned for its spicy kick, ginger doubles as a digestion-aiding dream-maker. By preventing discomfort, ginger ensures your body is at ease as you settle into sleep.

Turmeric Tea is a golden elixir with its active compound, curcumin. Beyond its anti-inflammatory prowess, curcumin contributes to a healthy sleep routine.

Hops Tea is the same hops that flavors your favorite brew. Did you know hops can also flavor your dreams? Hops create a mild sedative effect, promoting relaxation and easing anxiety.

Catnip Tea, from the plant *Nepeta cataria,* is often associated with feline delight. It contains nepetalactone, a compound that induces a sense of calm and relaxation.

California Poppy Tea, with its vibrant orange blooms, is nature's remedy for soothing the mind. It contains compounds that offer a gentle sedative effect, making it a delightful addition to your bedtime routine.

Lemon Verbena Tea is not the lemon fruit you may be thinking of. Lemon verbena is a flowering shrub native to South America with citrusy flavors that originate from the leaves. Lemon verbena extract has been studied to lower anxiety and reduce awakening in the night.

10 Recipes: Teas to Enhance Relaxation and Sleep Quality

We've got some great beginner recipes to help you sleep better. These flavorful blends not only taste amazing but also come with a bunch of benefits.

Chamomile Tea

Time: 10 minutes

Serving Time: Before bedtime

Prep Time: 5 minutes

Cook Time: 5 minutes

Ingredients

- 1 chamomile tea bag or 1 tbsp dried chamomile flowers
- 1 cup water
- honey or lemon (optional for taste)

Directions

1. Steep the chamomile tea bag or flowers in freshly boiled water for 5 minutes.
2. Add honey or lemon if desired.
3. Sip slowly and let the gentle chamomile embrace you with its soothing warmth.

Lavender Serenity Tea

Time: 15 minutes

Serving Time: Before bedtime

Prep Time: 5 minutes

Cook Time: 10 minutes

Ingredients

- 1 tsp dried lavender buds
- 1 chamomile tea bag
- 1 cup water
- splash of milk (optional)

Directions

1. Steep lavender buds and chamomile tea bag in freshly boiled water for 10 minutes.

2. Add a splash of milk for extra creaminess.

3. Sip and let the lavender-infused serenity prepare you for a restful sleep.

Valerian Root Tea

Time: 20 minutes

Serving Time: Before bedtime

Prep Time: 5 minutes

Cook Time: 15 minutes

Ingredients

- 1 tsp dried valerian root
- 1 tsp dried chamomile flowers
- 1 cup water
- dash of honey (optional)

Directions

1. Steep valerian root and chamomile flowers in freshly boiled water for 15 minutes.
2. Add a dash of honey if desired.
3. Sip slowly and feel the tranquil embrace of valerian root.

Passionflower Tea

Time: 15 minutes

Serving Time: Before bedtime

Prep Time: 5 minutes

Cook Time: 10 minutes

Ingredients

- 1 tsp dried passionflower
- 1 chamomile tea bag
- 1 cup water
- slice of orange (optional)

Directions

1. Steep dried passionflower and chamomile tea bag in freshly boiled water for 10 minutes.
2. Garnish with a slice of orange for a citrusy twist.
3. Sip and let the passionflower guide you into relaxation.

Lemon Balm Tea

Time: 15 minutes

Serving Time: Before bedtime

Prep Time: 5 minutes

Cook Time: 10 minutes

Ingredients

- 1 tbsp dried lemon balm leaves
- 1 chamomile tea bag
- 1 cup water
- drizzle of honey (optional)

Directions

1. Steep dried lemon balm leaves and chamomile tea bag in freshly boiled water for 10 minutes.
2. Add a drizzle of honey for sweetness.

3. Savor the refreshing lemon balm infusion as you prepare for a peaceful night.

Hops and Lavender Tea

Time: 20 minutes

Serving Time: Before bedtime

Prep Time: 5 minutes

Cook Time: 15 minutes

Ingredients

- 1 tsp dried hops
- 1 tsp dried lavender buds
- 1 chamomile tea bag
- 1 cup water

Directions

1. Steep dried hops, dried lavender buds, and chamomile tea bag in freshly boiled water for 15 minutes.
2. Strain and enjoy the twilight-infused serenity.
3. Let the calming blend of hops and lavender prepare you for a tranquil night's rest.

Vanilla Rooibos Tea

Time: 10 minutes

Serving Time: Before bedtime

Prep Time: 5 minutes

Cook Time: 5 minutes

Ingredients

- 1 vanilla rooibos tea bag
- 1 cup water
- splash of milk (optional)

Directions

1. Steep the vanilla rooibos tea bag in freshly boiled water for 5 minutes.
2. Add a splash of milk for a creamy touch.
3. Enjoy the sweet and soothing notes of vanilla rooibos as you wind down.

Ashwagandha Tri-Herb Sleep Tea

Time: 15 minutes

Serving Time: Before bedtime

Prep Time: 5 minutes

Cook Time: 10 minutes

Ingredients

- 1 tsp dried ashwagandha root pieces
- 1 tsp dried chamomile buds
- 1 tsp dried passionflower
- honey (optional)

Directions

1. Steep dried ashwagandha, chamomile, and passionflower in freshly boiled water for 10 minutes.

2. Strain and enjoy the aromatic dance of the herbs in your cup.

Golden Turmeric Tea

Time: 15 minutes

Serving Time: Before bedtime

Prep Time: 5 minutes

Cook Time: 10 minutes

Ingredients

- 1 tsp ground turmeric
- 1 tsp chamomile flowers
- 1 cup water
- sprinkle of black pepper and honey (optional)

Directions

1. Steep ground turmeric and chamomile flowers in freshly boiled water for 10 minutes.
2. Add a sprinkle of black pepper and honey for flavor.
3. Sip on the golden elixir and let the soothing properties of turmeric ease you into a tranquil night.

Lemon Verbena Tea

Time: 15 minutes

Serving Time: Before bedtime

Prep Time: 5 minutes

Cook Time: 10 minutes

Ingredients

- 1 tbsp dried lemon verbena leaves
- 1 tsp dried chamomile flowers
- 1 cup water
- slice of lemon (optional)

Directions

1. Steep dried lemon verbena leaves and chamomile in freshly boiled water for 10 minutes.

2. Garnish with a slice of lemon for a citrusy kick.

3. Enjoy the refreshing blend as you unwind for the night.

Berry Bedtime Tea

Time: 15 minutes

Serving Time: Before bedtime

Prep Time: 5 minutes

Cook Time: 10 minutes

Ingredients

- 1 tbsp mixed dried berries (blueberries, strawberries, or raspberries)
- 1 tsp dried chamomile flowers
- 1 cup water
- drizzle of honey (optional)

Directions

1. Steep mixed dried berries and chamomile in freshly boiled water for 10 minutes.

2. Strain.
3. Add a drizzle of honey for sweetness.
4. Savor the delightful berry infusion bedtime tea as you prepare for a serene night's rest.

Tips: Setting a Bedtime Tea Ritual

Setting a bedtime routine can be a game-changer for a good night's sleep. Giving your body a little heads-up that it's time to wind down and get cozy could be what you've been missing. If you're tired of tossing and turning or just want to upgrade your sleep game, here are eight simple and fuss-free tips to create a bedtime routine that'll have you snoozing like a champ.

Maintain a Consistent Sleep Schedule

Keep it steady! Try to hit the hay and wake up at the same time every day, even on weekends. It helps regulate your body's internal clock.

Do a Digital Detox Before Bed

Give those screens a break about 30 minutes before bedtime. The blue light can mess with your melatonin levels, making it harder to catch those Zs.

Create a Cozy Sleep Environment

Make your sleep space a haven. Dim the lights, keep the room cool, and invest in some comfy bedding. It's all about setting the stage for quality rest.

Choose Wind-Down Activities

Find your chill zone before bedtime. Whether it's reading a book, listening to calming music, or doing some light stretching, find activities that help you relax.

There are many natural ways to help ease the process of menopause, but one thing that helps immensely is using the healing power of tea, which, thankfully is cheap and flavorful. Again, just like menstrual relief, it's best to consult with a doctor beforehand to ensure these natural remedies are suited for you.

Black Cohosh Root Tea is known to reduce vaginal dryness and hot flashes. Usually, it is recommended for early menopause, but make sure you're not consuming it if you're pregnant or being treated for liver disease or high blood pressure. Side effects can cause nausea, upset stomach, muscle aches, skin rashes, breast pain, and vaginal bleeding at random intervals.

Ginseng Tea alleviates several menopause symptoms such as hot flashes and night sweats. It is also highly beneficial for osteopenia and lessens the risk of cardiovascular diseases for women. It can even increase the sexual drive of women. Unfortunately, mixing ginseng with some medications can cause jitteriness and headaches.

Chasteberry Tea treats premenstrual symptoms and maintains a balance between estrogen and progesterone, which helps in a smooth transition from perimenopause to menopause. However, if you're on antipsychotic medication, birth control, or hormone replacement therapy, then this should be avoided. For any hormone-sensitive disease, chasteberry should be strictly avoided.

Red Raspberry Leaf Tea does not have a specific link to symptoms of menopause. However, it can lessen the heavy flow that comes with perimenopause. The only disadvantage is the tendency of the leaves to cause loose stools and increase urination.

Red Clover Tea gets rid of hot flashes and night sweats in menopause. On top of that, it boosts immunity, improves bone strength, and helps with high blood pressure. Additionally, red clover may lessen anxiety, depression, and even vaginal dryness. However, rarely, it can cause headaches and nausea.

Dong Quai Tea Pelvic pain during menopause? Try Dong Quai tea. This Chinese herb regulates estrogen levels and also regulates menstrual cycle, therefore lessening cramps. When mixed with chamomile tea, it can reduce hot flashes. This tea should be avoided in case of a carrot family allergy.

Valerian Root Tea has the ability to reduce hot flashes and treat anxiety, stress, insomnia, and depression makes this an excellent tea. It can also help with PMS symptoms.

Licorice Tea can reduce stress and hot flashes. It may also improve respiratory health, is an anti-inflammatory, has antimicrobial effects, and aids digestion.

Green Tea is highly effective for bone health and reducing inflammation. The antioxidants and caffeine in green tea can help boost metabolism and slow weight gain. However, too much green tea means too much caffeine, which can disturb sleep patterns and cause headaches.

Ginkgo Biloba Tea, with it's fan shaped leaves, is a wonderful hormone-balancing herb. Ginkgo helps with increasing estrogen levels and calming mood swings. Furthermore, Gingko increases blood flow.

Men's Health: Testosterone Balance and Prostate Health

As a man, you might not be open to discussing sensitive health topics, primarily hormonal imbalances that interfere with your physical and sexual functioning. But did you know you can work on these problems with the healing power of herbal teas? All you

Directions

1. Wash your fresh ginger and cut it into thin slices.
2. In a saucepan, add the ginger and some water.
3. Bring the mixture to a boil over the flame. Reduce the heat.
4. Simmer for 5–10 minutes, depending on how strong you want your tea.
5. Pour the tea through a fine strainer to catch the ginger.
6. Serve your tea with lemon for some complementary acidity.
7. Add a drizzle of honey.
8. For additional yumminess, add cinnamon or mint.

Raspberry Leaf Tea

Time: 15 minutes

Serving Time: Anytime

Prep Time: 5 minutes

Cook Time: 10 minutes

Ingredients

- 1 cup of water
- 1 tbsp loose and dried raspberry leaf
- honey (optional)
- orange or lemon slice

Directions

1. Boil some water and let it cool for a few minutes.
2. Add 1 tbsp of loose red raspberry leaf tea to a tea infuser

or bag. (You can make it in a pot with loose tea, which can be sieved.)

3. Place your tea infuser or tea bag in your cup and pour hot water over it.
4. Add a slice of orange or lemon.
5. Let the tea steep for 5–10 minutes
6. Remove the tea bag, and your tea is ready.
7. Add honey to your liking.
8. If you want your tea iced, you can follow the same steps but pour it over ice after it has been allowed to cool a bit.

Ashwagandha Tea

Time: 12 minutes

Serving Time: Anytime

Prep Time: 2 minutes

Cook Time: 10 minutes

Ingredients

- 1 cup of water
- 1 tsp dried ashwagandha root
- honey (optional
- turmeric (optional)
- cinnamon (optional)

Directions

1. Boil 1 cup of water in a saucepan.
2. Add 1 tsp of dried ashwagandha root.
3. Cover the boiling water with a lid and lower the flame.
4. Let the water simmer for 10 minutes.

5. Remove the water from the stove and allow the tea to cool.
6. Use a strainer to gently pour the water into a cup or mug.
7. Add turmeric, cinnamon, honey, or other sweeteners for enhanced flavor.

Ginkgo Biloba Tea

Time: 5 minutes

Serving Time: Anytime

Prep Time: 1 minute

Cook Time: 4 minutes

Ingredients

- 1 tbsp dried ginkgo biloba leaves
- 1 cup of water
- honey (optional)

Directions

1. Put 2 cups of water in a saucepan and let it boil.
2. Add the tea leaves to the water and let it simmer.
3. Strain the tea.
4. Add honey to your taste.

Valerian Root Tea

Time: 5 minutes

Serving Time: Anytime

Prep Time: 2 minutes

Cook Time: 3 minutes

The Green Glow

Ingredients

- 1 tsp valerian root
- 1 cup of water
- 2 tbsp honey
- 1 tsp lemon juice

Directions

1. Steep the valerian root for 2–3 minutes.
2. Strain your tea.
3. Sweeten with honey and add a teaspoon of lemon.

Chamomile Tea

Time: 10 minutes

Serving Time: Anytime

Prep Time: 3 minutes

Cook Time: 7 minutes

Ingredients

- 1 cup of water
- 1 tbsp dried chamomile
- honey (optional)

Directions

1. Use a saucepan and start boiling water on high heat.
2. Once the water begins to boil, turn off the heat and add the dried chamomile tea.
3. Keep it covered with a lid for a minute.
4. Strain the chamomile tea into the cup.

5. Add honey to taste and serve.

Nettle Tea

Time: 10 minutes

Serving Time: Anytime

Prep Time: 2 minutes

Cook Time: 8 minutes

Ingredients

- 1 cup of water
- 1 tbsp dried nettle leaves
- pinch of cinnamon (optional)
- honey (optional)

Directions

1. Boil some water in a saucepan.
2. Add the nettle leaves to the water.
3. Let it simmer for a couple of minutes, and then turn off the stove.
4. Let the tea sit for some minutes and then strain it.
5. For additional flavor, you can add cinnamon and honey as a sweetener.

Red Clover Tea

Time: 12 minutes

Serving Time: Anytime

Prep Time: 2 minutes

Cook Time: 10 minutes

The Green Glow

Ingredients

- 1 tbsp dried red clover blossom
- 1 cup of water
- 1 tbsp fresh mint leaves
- honey (optional)

Directions

1. To make the tea, boil some water.
2. Add the dried red clover blossom and mint.
3. Let the herbs simmer for about 10 minutes.
4. Strain the tea.
5. Add honey for sweetness to your taste.

Tips for Both Genders

- Once you start taking a specific tea, make sure you make it regularly, as many herbal teas take time to show any effect.
- Always consult your doctor before starting to consume any herbal tea. Many of them can turn harmful if mixed with certain medications.
- Talk to your healthcare professional because herbal tea can affect you negatively if you have an allergy to certain herbs or if you have certain medical conditions.
- Take the proper herb dosage in your tea, as excess can have side effects.
- Adding two different blends can provide more benefits than just one herbal tea.
- If teas are not your preference, you can add the herbs to your routine in other ways, such as in the form of supplements or tinctures.

Chapter 7

Skin and Hair

Taking care of your skin and hair is incredibly important for your overall health. When you have vibrant skin and hair, it not only boosts your confidence but also shows strong inner vitality because outer health reflects inner health.

Your skin is the largest organ in your body and acts as a barrier against environmental factors such as pollution, UV rays, and bacteria. By maintaining a good skincare routine, you can keep your skin clean, hydrated, and protected. Plus, healthy skin can improve your immune system and reduce the risk of infections.

Now, onto hair. Your hair is also a reflection of your inner health. When you take care of your hair, you're also taking care of your scalp. A clean scalp promotes hair growth and prevents issues such as dandruff and itchiness. Regularly washing and conditioning keeps hair moisturized and prevents breakage. Additionally, a healthy diet and proper hydration contribute to shiny, strong, and luscious locks.

However, it's not just about the external benefits. When you invest time and effort into your skincare and haircare routines, it can become a form of self-care. Turning your hair regimen into a self-care ritual allows you to relax, unwind, and pamper yourself. Taking care of your skin and hair can also boost your self-esteem, thus improving your mental well-being.

So, by prioritizing skincare and haircare, you can improve your overall health, protect yourself from external factors, and boost your confidence. It's all about finding a routine that works for you and sticking to it. Remember, self-care is not selfish; it's essential.

Herbal Teas That Promote Radiant Hair and Skin.

Here are several powerful, nourishing herbal teas you can incorporate into your beauty routine. Remember, it's also important to eat a balanced diet, stay hydrated, and protect your skin and hair from environmental damage.

Horsetail Tea is known by the latin name *Equisetum arvense*. Horsetail has been widely used in traditional medicine traditions for supporting hair health. The herb horsetail contains high levels of silica- which encourages blood flow to the scalp and strengthens hair follicles. Silica is also extremely supportive of good bone health.

Nettle Tea comes from the plant *Urtica dioica* which is commonly called stinging nettle due to the stinging hairs on the leaves and stems. Don't let the name scare you because the stinging compounds are neutralized after just a few seconds of being exposed to freshly boiled water. Nettles are very high in minerals that are necessary for glowing skin and strong hair.

Bhringaraj Tea hails from India and can also be called False Daisy if you find the authentic name hard to pronounce. False Daisy is otherwise known as *Eclipta prostrata* and comes from the sunflower family.

Rose Hips Tea is a potent source of vitamin C, an antioxidant that protects the skin from damage from free radicals. The higher the reserves of antioxidants in the body, the more protected your skin will be from factors that age or damage it.

Amla Tea is otherwise known as Indian Gooseberry. Indian gooseberries are green, sour, and tart. Interestingly, in a study of 17 different herbs, amla was found to be the second most potent inhibitor of hair loss caused by a common hormone that causes increased shedding called DHT. DHT is responsible for many cases of hair loss in men and women.

Green Tea supports skin health through it's high antioxidant content. Abundant reservoirs of antioxidants in the skin guard against wrinkles, fine lines, and loss of collagen. Green tea has been observed to suppress melanin secretion, minimizing sun spots and age spots.

7 Recipes: Blends to Enhance Skin Glow and Hair Health

The following recipes will help enhance the glow of your skin and make your hair healthy

Green Tea and Lemon

Time: 4 minutes

Serving Time: Anytime

Prep Time: 2 minutes

Cook Time: 2 minutes

Ingredients

- 1 tsp dried green tea leaves
- lemon juice, to taste

The Green Glow

- 1 cup of water

Directions

1. Boil a cup of water and turn off the heat. Add the green tea leaves and let them steep for 2 minutes.
2. Strain you tea.
3. Add fresh lemon juice to taste for a boost of skin-loving antioxidants.

Nettle Rose Tea

Time: 7 minutes

Serving Time: Anytime

Prep Time: 2 minutes

Cook Time: 5 minutes

Ingredients

- 1 cup of water
- 1 tsp dried nettle leaves
- 1 tsp dried rose hips
- honey, to taste

Directions

1. Boil a cup of water and turn off the heat.
2. Add a teaspoon of dried nettle leaf and a teaspoon of dried rose hips and let them steep for 5 minutes.
3. Strain and add honey to your taste.

False Daisy Tea

Time: 7 minutes

Serving Time: Anytime

Prep Time: 2 minutes

Cook Time: 5 minutes

Ingredients

- 1 cup of water
- 1 tsp dried false daisy
- honey, to taste

Directions

1. Boil a cup of water and turn off the heat once boiled.
2. Add your dried false daisy to steep for 5 minutes.
3. Strain your tea.
4. Add honey to taste.

Rose Green Tea

Time: 4 minutes

Serving Time: Anytime

Prep Time: 2 minutes

Cook Time: 2 minutes

Ingredients

- 1 cup of water
- 1 tsp dried green tea leaves
- 1 tsp dried rose hips

Directions

1. Boil 1 cup of water and turn off the heat once boiled.

2. Add 1 tsp of dried rose hips and 1 tsp dried green tea leaves into the pot.
3. Strain your tea.
4. Enjoy your tea right away for an antioxidant-rich brew to nourish your skin.

Amla Mint Tea

Time: 4 minutes

Serving Time: Anytime

Prep Time: 2 minutes

Cook Time: 2 minutes

Ingredients

- 1 tsp amla powder
- 1 cup of water
- several fresh mint leaves
- honey, to taste

Directions

1. Boil 1 cup of water on the stovetop. Once boiled, turn off the heat.
2. Stir in 1 teaspoon of amla powder and toss in a few fresh mint leaves. Allow to steep for 2 minutes.
3. Strain your tea and enjoy.

Horsetail Chai Tea

Time: 9 minutes

Serving Time: Anytime

Prep Time: 4 minutes

Cook Time: 5 minutes

Ingredients

- 1 cup of water
- 1 tsp dried horsetail
- 1 clove
- 1 cardamom pod
- pinch of ground cinnamon and ground ginger
- honey, to taste

Directions

1. Take 1 clove and a cardamom pod and grind fresh with a mortar and pestal or throw into a spice grinder and pulse for a few seconds. Add half of this powder to you freshly boiled water along with a pinch of ground cinnamon and ginger.
2. Add in your dried horsetail powder and allow to steep for 5 minutes.
3. Strain your tea and enjoy this warming, cozy brew that encourages thick, strong hair.

Ayurvedic Hair Growth Tea

Time: 8 minutes

Serving Time: Anytime

Prep Time: 3 minutes

Cook Time: 5 minutes

Ingredients

- 1 tsp amla powder
- 1 cup of water

- 1 tsp dried false daisy
- a pinch of dried, ground ginger
- honey, to taste

Directions

1. Boil a cup of water on the stovetop and once boiled turn off the heat.
2. Stir in a teaspoon of amla powder and add a teaspoon of dried false daisy. Add a pinch of ground, dried ginger root.
3. Steep the herbs for 5 minutes and then strain.
4. Add honey to taste and savor this brew composed of traditional Indian herbs for growing your locks long and healthy.

Tips: Integrating Teas Into Daily Beauty Routines

Integrating teas into your daily beauty routine can be a fantastic way to enhance your skincare and haircare. Here are some tips on how to incorporate teas into your beauty routine.

- **Facial steam:** Start your skincare routine by steaming your face with herbal tea. Boil some water, pour it into a bowl, and add rose hips, green tea, or other relaxing aromatic herbs of your choosing. Lean over the bowl, cover your head with a towel, and let the steam open up your pores for a deep cleanse.
- **Toner:** After cleansing, use cooled herbal tea as a natural toner. Green tea or rosewater tea can work wonders for balancing the skin's pH, reducing redness, and tightening pores. Apply it with a cotton pad or transfer it to a spray bottle for a refreshing mist.

- **Eye treatment:** Place cooled green or black tea bags over your eyes to reduce swelling and soothe tired eyes. The anti-inflammatory properties of these teas can help alleviate dark circles and promote a brighter appearance.
- **Face mask:** Mix herbal tea, such as matcha or rooibos, with honey or yogurt to create a nourishing face mask. Apply it to your face, leave it on for 10–15 minutes, and rinse off with warm water. This DIY mask can revitalize your skin and leave it feeling soft and supple.
- **Lip scrub:** Mix a teaspoon of antioxidant-rich matcha powder with honey and sugar to create a gentle lip scrub. Gently apply the mixture onto your lips to eliminate dead skin cells and reveal smoother, softer lips.
- **Bath soak:** Add a few tea bags or loose tea leaves to your bathwater for a relaxing and aromatic experience. Try herb-infused epsom salts such as lavender, chamomile, or jasmine to help calm your mind, soothe your skin, and create a spa-like ambiance.

Don't forget, these tips are just a starting point. Feel free to get creative and experiment with different teas to find what works best for you. Cheers to a beautiful and tea-infused beauty routine!

How to Use Herbal Tea For Your Hair

Remember, everyone's hair is unique, so feel free to experiment with different herbal teas and find what works best for you. Incorporating herbal tea into your haircare routine can be super beneficial.

- **Herbal tea rinse:** Brew a strong cup of herbal tea, such as chamomile, rosemary, or nettle. Let it cool down and use it as a final hair rinse after shampooing. Then, pour the tea over your hair, making sure to saturate your scalp and strands. Leave it on for a few minutes, then rinse it out with cool water. This can help nourish your hair, add shine, and promote a healthy scalp.

- **Scalp massage:** Brew a cup of herbal tea, such as peppermint or lavender, and let it cool. After that, transfer the tea to a spray bottle and add some drops of essential oil, if desired. Section your hair and spritz the tea onto your scalp. Massage your head in circular motions for a few minutes to stimulate blood flow and promote hair growth. Leave it on for a while, then rinse it out.

- **Hair mask:** Create a DIY hair mask by mixing herbal tea with natural ingredients like honey, coconut oil, or aloe vera gel. For example, you can blend hibiscus tea with yogurt and honey to create a nourishing mask for dry hair. Apply the mask to your head, focusing on the tips of the hair, and let it sit for 20–30 minutes. Rinse it out thoroughly and enjoy the benefits of hydrated and revitalized hair.

- **Leave-in conditioner:** Brew a cup of herbal tea, such as green tea or chamomile, and let it cool. Then, pour the tea into a spray bottle and add some essential oil. After washing your hair, spritz the tea onto damp hair as a leave-in conditioner. It can help detangle your hair, reduce frizz, and add a natural shine.

Chapter 8

Pain Relief and Inflammation

I
f you have spent a good deal of time on this earth, you have likely felt aches and pains. We are talking about body aches and pains you acquire because of natural wear and tear on the body, age, or perhaps certain hobbies or occupations that are hard on the musculoskeletal system.

You might be wondering why you feel body pain and we are here to help give you a better understanding. But don't worry, we're not here to pull out complicated terms and cause confusion. We'll be discussing some natural ways that can help your body fight pain and inflammation.

The Science of Pain and Inflammation

All right, let's start with a little bit of the science behind pain and inflammation, those two tagalongs symptoms that often come uninvited. Pain, in its essence, is like our body's way of saying "Hey, we've got an issue here!" Whether it's a stubbed toe or a more serious injury, pain ensures you pay attention and take the necessary actions. Inflammation is your body's attempt to start fixing things.

The classic signs of inflammation include:

- redness
- heat
- swelling
- pain

These signs are indicative of the body's efforts to heal itself. Redness and heat result from increased blood flow to the affected area. Swelling occurs due to the accumulation of fluid and immune cells, and pain serves as a warning signal to prevent further damage.

In summary, inflammation is a protective and healing response that the body employs to maintain its integrity and overcome challenges. While acute inflammation is a beneficial and necessary process, chronic inflammation, lasting for an extended period, can contribute to various health conditions.

Certain herbs have anti-inflammatory properties that can help dial down the inflammation response. Additionally, some herbs have analgesic properties, meaning they can help alleviate pain. So, sipping on a cup of herbal tea is a good strategy to give your body a little extra support during healing.

Herbal Soothers and Anti-Inflammatory Agents

Herbs are nature's toolbox for soothing and easing pain in your body. Packed with tons of natural healing compounds, they bring relief swiftly. Making a cup of herbal tea is always a good choice for your body, using simple plant power to help you feel better.

Turmeric Tea is a golden spice powerhouse in the herbal kingdom. Turmeric has an active compound called curcumin which is renowned for its potent anti-inflammatory and antioxidant properties. Turmeric has been a staple in traditional medicine for centuries, and modern research backs up its ability to alleviate pain and reduce inflammation.

Ginger Tea is not just a zesty addition to your tea, ginger packs a punch when it comes to fighting inflammation. Its bioactive compound, gingerol, is known for its anti-inflammatory and analgesic effects.

Chamomile Tea is known for its calming effects, however did you know chamomile is a gentle anti-inflammatory? Chamomile's essential oils and antioxidants can help soothe irritated tissues and ease discomfort.

Frankincense Tea is often overshadowed by its more famous cousin, myrrh. However, frankincense is great for reducing inflammation. Resin of frankincense contains boswellic acids, which have anti-inflammatory properties.

Arnica Tea is a bright yellow flower that is nature's own anti-inflammatory powerhouse.-Arnica is also known as wolf's bane or mountain tobacco.

Devil's Claw Tea might have an ominous name, however devil's claw is a natural anti-inflammatory used for centuries in traditional medicine. The roots contain compounds called iridoid glycosides that may help reduce pain and inflammation, making it a great choice for those looking for some relief from musculoskeletal pain.

White Willow Bark Tea is nature's aspirin. This isn't just a figure of speech since aspirin was, in fact, derived from this botanical. White willow bark contains salicin, a natural compound with anti-inflammatory and pain-relieving properties.

Jamaican Dogwood Tea is a deciduous tropical tree native to Jamaica, Haiti, Florida, and Central America. Jamaican dogwood is an excellent pain-fighting botanical. Be advised that Jamaican dogwood is not known for its superb flavor and can cause a tingling sensation in the mouth.

7 Recipes: Teas Focused on Pain Alleviation and Reducing Inflammation

Get ready to sip your way to soothing bliss with our collection of 7 herbal tea recipes tailored for the task of easing pain and calming inflammation. These aren't your average teas, they're a comforting blend of natural healers, each crafted to bring a touch of relief to your day.

Ginger Green Tea

Prep Time: 5 minutes

Cook Time: 7 minutes

Ingredients

- 1 tbsp fresh ginger, sliced
- 1 tsp honey (optional)
- 1 lemon wedge
- 1 cup of water
- 1 tsp dried green tea leaves

Directions

1. Bring water to a boil and add fresh ginger.
2. Simmer for 7 minutes.
3. Strain into a cup, add honey if desired, and steep the green tea bag for an extra layer of flavor.

Arnica Tea

Prep Time: 5 minutes

Cook Time: 7 minutes

Ingredients

- 1 tsp dried arnica flowers
- 1 cup of water
- honey, to taste

Directions

1. Bring a cup of water to boil on your stovetop. Once boiled, turn off the heat.
2. Add dried arnica leaves and steep for 7 minutes.
3. Strain into a cup, add honey if desired, and enjoy this delightful yellow tea.

White Willow Tea

Prep Time: 5 minutes

Cook Time: 5 minutes

Ingredients

- 1 tsp dried white willow bark
- 1 cup of water
- 1 tsp chamomile flowers
- honey, to taste

Directions

1. Bring a cup of water to a boil and then turn off the heat.

2. Add dried white willow bark and chamomile flowers. Steep for 5 minutes.
3. Strain into a cup and add honey to taste.

Jamaican Dogwood Tea

Prep Time: 5 minutes

Cook Time: 5 minutes

Ingredients

- 1 tsp dried jamaican dogwood
- 1 cup of water
- 1 tsp dried licorice root
- a pinch of cinnamon
- honey, to taste

Directions

1. Bring a cup of water to a boil and then turn off the heat.
2. Add dried jamaican dogwood and licorice and steep for 5 minutes. Add a pinch of cinnamon for taste.
3. Strain into a cup and add honey to your preferred taste.

Devil's Claw Tea

Prep Time: 5 minutes

Cook Time: 5 minutes

Ingredients

- 1 tsp dried devil's claw root
- 1 cup of water
- honey, to taste

Directions

1. Bring a cup of water to a boil and then turn off the heat.
2. Add dried devil's claw and steep for 5 minutes.
3. Strain into a cup and add honey. Honey is recommended since this herb has a bitter taste.

Frankincense White Tea

Prep Time: 5 minutes

Cook Time: 5 minutes

Ingredients

- 1 tsp frankincense resin
- 1 cup of water
- honey, to taste
- 1 tsp dried white tea leaves
- 1 tsp dried lemon verbena leaves

Directions

1. Bring a cup of water to a boil and then turn off the heat.

2. Add the frankincense resin, white tea leaves, and lemon verbena. Steep for 5 minutes.

3. Strain into a cup and add honey.

Turmeric Tea

Prep Time: 5 minutes

Cook Time: 7 minutes

Ingredients

- 1 tsp ground turmeric

- 1 tsp honey (optional)
- 1 lemon wedge
- 1 cup milk
- 1 tsp black tea leaves

Directions

1. Bring milk to simmer, not a boil. Turn off the heat and add your black tea leaves and ground turmeric.
2. Simmer for 7 minutes.
3. Strain into a cup, add honey or lemon if desired.

You can easily customize these teas according to your taste. Also consider adding these to your nighttime routine. They are perfect to consume at night time as your body recovers naturally during your sleep.

Tips: Brewing Techniques for Maximum Relief

Brewing the perfect cup of herbal is a simple art that can unlock the full potential of nature's healing bounty.

Use Filtered Water

Start with clean, filtered water to ensure the purest taste and avoid any unwanted impurities that might interfere with the healing properties or taste of the herbs.

Steep for Adequate Time

Different herbs release their beneficial compounds at varying rates. Follow the recommended steeping times to allow the herbs to fully infuse into the water. Longer steeping times can enhance the extraction of medicinal properties.

Use the Optimal Temperature

Pay attention to water temperature. Some delicate herbs, such as green tea and certain flowers, benefit from lower temperatures to preserve their therapeutic properties. Boiling water may be suitable for heartier herbs such as ginger or turmeric.

Cover While Steeping

Covering your tea while it steeps helps to trap essential oils and prevent the escape of aromatic compounds. This ensures that you get the full spectrum of flavors and therapeutic benefits in your cup.

Customize With Honey

Add a teaspoon of raw honey to your herbal tea. Not only does it sweeten the brew, but honey also offers its own set of natural healing properties, contributing to the overall relief.

Incorporate Citrus

A splash of citrus, such as lemon or orange, not only adds a refreshing twist but also brings additional vitamin C and antioxidants, enhancing the immune-boosting properties of your herbal tea.

Experiment With Combinations

Don't be afraid to experiment with different herb combinations. Some herbs work synergistically, enhancing each other's benefits. For example, combining chamomile and lavender can enhance relaxation.

Sip Mindfully

Take a moment to engage in mindful sipping. Close your eyes, inhale the aroma, and sip slowly. This mindful approach can enhance the overall experience and promote relaxation, both mentally and physically.

Consider Cold Infusions

Experiment with cold infusions, especially during hot weather. Cold brewing can be gentler on certain herbs, preserving their delicate flavors and medicinal properties without exposing them to high temperatures.

Remember, the key is to enjoy the process of making and drinking your herbal tea. You can utilize these tips to your preferences and discover what works best for you in creating a soothing and therapeutic cup.

Chapter 9

Energy and Focus

Ever find yourself yearning for that extra burst of vitality to power through a hectic day? Energy drinks can be a tempting option, but let's face it: are most of them really all that healthy? The obvious answer is a resounding *no*. Sure, they may offer a quick fix, but the sugar crashes and mysterious chemical blends may cause more harm than good.

Tea is a shining star yet again—and no, it doesn't have to be your grandmother's formal, lace-and-cup ritual. A quick, simple cup of nature's wonder is all you need. In this chapter, we'll be detailing how tea can be the energy boost you've been looking for.

We've all had the feeling of an afternoon slump after we've eaten lunch or even a small snack. Teas, beyond being your cozy beverage companions, contain natural compounds that can give your metabolism a friendly nudge. But what is "metabolism". We'll give you the super simple explanation.

Metabolism is regulated by a network of enzymes and hormones, and it is influenced by factors such as age, gender, genetics, and overall health. The rate of metabolism, often referred to as metabolic rate, determines how efficiently the body utilizes energy and plays a crucial role in maintaining homeostasis.

Simple enough, right? Now, let's get into how we can naturally give ourselves a boost.

Herbs That Boost Energy and Focus

The botanical world is filled with hundreds and thousands of herbs, both discovered and undiscovered. Out of these, many contain unique blends of minerals and chemicals that help your body boost energy and help you create focus mindsets.

With extensive research and exploring the rare underground herbs, here is a compilation of some of the best mind-boosting and energizing herbs for you:

Rosemary Tea, otherwise known as *Salvia rosamarinus,* is first on the list. This little sprig packs a punch of endorphin-stimulating chemicals, revving up your vitality naturally. Rosemary contains active compounds such as triterpenes and phenolic acids, including: rosmarinic acid, carnosic acid, rosmanol, carnosol, ursolic acid, and betulinic acid. These compounds stimulate blood flow, enhancing oxygen delivery to your brain and muscles and boosting energy from within.

Sage Tea is packed with antioxidants and compounds that support improved cognitive function, sage can help kick that fatigue to the curb. Sage also contains phytoestrogens that stimulate estrogen receptors, assisting with menstrual cycle-related fatigue.

Ginseng Tea has long been one of the hidden herbal gems to come from Asia. This ancient root has been boosting energy for centuries, and it's not just folklore. Packed with adaptogens, ginseng helps your body adapt to stress, giving you sustained energy without the jitters.

Gotu Kola Tea has been a part of Indian Ayurvedic, traditional Chinese, and Indonesian medicine for a long time. Some parts of the world even refer to this as the "herb of longevity," as it has strong immune-stabilizing and energy-boosting properties. Packed with adaptogens and antioxidants, gotu kola has a knack for combating fatigue and promoting mental alertness. Gotu kola has been shown in research to increase blood flow to the brain.

Ginkgo Tea is one of the oldest spices in the world and has been used in brewing tea and other herbal as well as medicinal mixes. Research suggests that ginkgo enhances blood flow, delivering a power-packed oxygen supply to your brain and body.

Matcha Tea is one of the highest caffeine-containing herbs on Earth. Packed with L-theanine and other antioxidants, this herb is considered a real powerhouse. The active components of matcha induce a state of calm alertness that promotes sustained focus and cognitive clarity. L-theanine, combined with matcha's caffeine, creates a unique synergy, enhancing attention and memory.

Black Tea is full of potent antioxidants, particularly theaflavins and catechins, are known for their cognitive-enhancing properties. Black tea also has caffeine which supports energy levels. These compounds have been linked to improved brain function, increased alertness, and enhanced focus. Regular consumption of black tea has shown positive effects on attention and memory.

Pu-erh Tea stands out as a cognitive champion in the herbal tea realm. Pu-erh tea is fermented tea and the fermentation process yields many health-giving compounds. Packed with polyphenols and theanine, it unleashes a dual action of antioxidant protection and calming focus. The theanine content promotes a state of alert relaxation, fostering sustained attention without the jitters. Pu-erh's unique microbial fermentation process further contributes to its brain-boosting potential.

10 Recipes: Energizing Blends for Increased Focus and Stamina

Although the herbal benefits of roots and leaves are best taken when consumed raw, their concoctions can also be helpful. Especially when simmered over low flame with proper ingredients. This will not only boost the taste but also get rid of the unwanted chemicals and bacteria that might have held onto them in their natural habitats.

So, without further chit-chat, let's get to the next step of our herbal understanding: the practical work of how to make energy-boosting and focus-generating drinks out of them!

Rosemary Booster

Time: 5 minutes

Serving Time: Dinner

Prep Time: 2 minutes

Cook Time: 3 minutes

Ingredients

- 1 cup of water
- 2–4 rosemary sprigs
- lemon juice

Directions

1. Boil a cup of water in a kettle or in a pot on the stovetop.
2. Add the rosemary sprigs and allow it to stand for 3 minutes so the taste can blend in.
3. Add lemon juice for taste enhancement and it's ready to drink!

Black Chai Tea

Time: 8 minutes

Serving Time: Anytime

Prep Time: 2 minutes

Cook Time: 5 minutes

Ingredients

- 1 cup of water
- 1 tsp dried black tea leaves
- ½ tsp chai spice powder
- splash of milk
- sugar (as per taste)

Directions

1. Boil your cup of water and then turn off the heat.
2. Add your black tea leaves and steep for 5 minutes. Add in chai spice powder.
3. Strain your tea and add a splash of milk and sugar to your taste.

Pro tip: If you wish to make it more tempting, try adding multiple spices such as cardamom, cinnamon, ginger, or cloves to get an extra boost!

Matcha Mix

Time: 5 minutes

Serving Time: Morning

Prep Time: 2 minutes

Cook Time: 5 minutes

The Green Glow

Ingredients

- ¼ tsp matcha powder
- 2 tbsp water
- 1 cup steamed milk
- sweetener (honey or maple syrup)

Directions

1. Sift the matcha powder in a small bowl.
2. Add water and blend it with matcha together until a foam is formed.
3. Add steamed milk and mix.
4. You can add the sweetener of your choice to adjust the bitterness as per your taste.

Yerba Mate Infusion

Time: 15 minutes

Serving Time: When you need to have a good concentration

Prep Time: 5 minutes

Cook Time: 10 minutes

Ingredients

- 1 cup of water
- 1 tsp dried yerba mate leaves
- lemon wedge
- honey or sugar, to taste

Directions

1. Boil your water.

2. Add yerba leaves and let them sit in boiling water for 10 minutes. Cover the kettle.
3. Once infused, strain the tea.
4. Add lemon and sugar for taste, and it's done!

Pro tip: You can also make it iced by cooling the infusion and adding ice cubes and the sweetener of your choice! Both blends work great for increasing stamina and focus.

Ginkgo Masala

Time: 10 minutes

Serving Time: Morning and afternoon

Prep Time: 2 minutes

Cook Time: 8 minutes

Ingredients

- 1 tsp dried ginkgo biloba tea leaves or 1 ginkgo tea bag
- 1 black tea bag
- 1 cup water
- ½ cup milk (adjust to taste)
- 1–2 tbsp honey or sweetener of choice (optional)
- masala mix containing ¼ teaspoon ground cardamom and ginger, ⅛ teaspoon cloves and black pepper, and ½ teaspoon ground cinnamon

Directions

1. Make the spice blend.
2. Boil a cup of water and take off the heat once boiled. Steep the ginkgo leaves and for 4 minutes.
3. Add your spice mix and black tea and steep for another 4 minutes.

4. Add milk to taste.
5. Strain the tea and done!

Sage Tea

Time: 7 minutes

Serving Time: Morning and night

Prep Time: 2 minutes

Cook Time: 5 minutes

Ingredients

- 1 tsp fresh sage leaves
- 1 cup of water
- honey or lemon to taste (optional)

Directions

1. If using fresh sage leaves, rinse them thoroughly. If using dried sage leaves, measure out 1 tsp.
2. Bring 1 cup of water to a boil.
3. Put the fresh or dried sage leaves in a teapot. Steep for 5-minutes.
4. Strain the tea and add the sweetener of your choice.
5. Serve and enjoy.

Ginseng Brew

Time: 1 hour

Serving Time: Night

Prep Time: 15 minutes

Cook Time: 10 minutes

Ingredients

- ginseng root cut in ½–¼ in. pieces
- 1 cup of water
- lemon wedge

Directions

1. Cut the ginseng into cubes.
2. Put ginseng and rice in a pan and roast them.
3. Put the water in and boil it on low flame for 10 minutes on low heat.
4. Strain it and add a few drops of lemon for taste and it's ready to drink!

Gotu Kola Delight

Time: 15–20 minutes

Serving Time: Morning

Prep Time: 5 minutes

Cook Time: 15 minutes

Ingredients

- 1 tsp dried gotu kola leaves
- ½ tsp dried lavender
- ½ tsp dried chamomile buds
- 1 cup of water
- honey, to taste

The Green Glow

Directions

1. Boil one cup of water in a kettle or pot on your stovetop. Turn off the heat once boiled.
2. Mix the herbs in with the freshly boiled water.
3. Simmer for 15–20 minutes.
4. Strain and it's ready to drink!

Pu-erh Chai Mix

Time: 5–7 minutes

Serving Time: Anytime

Prep Time: 2 minutes

Cook Time: 5 minutes

Ingredients

- chai mix containing a pinch of cinnamon, ½ tsp ginger, ¼ tsp cardamom, a pinch of nutmeg, and black pepper (1–2 tbsp of this mix)
- 1 tsp dried pu-erh leaves
- 1 cup of water
- ½ cup milk (dairy or non-dairy)
- sweetener of your choice (honey, sugar, maple syrup, etc.)

Directions

1. Heat 1 cup of water in a pot until it reaches a rolling boil.
2. Add the chai mix and pu-erh to the boiling water and lower heat to a simmer for 5–7 minutes.
3. Add ½ cup of milk.
4. Strain and serve.

Green Tea

Time: 5 minutes

Serving Time: Anytime but best after a meal

Prep Time: 2 minutes

Cook Time: 3 minutes

Ingredients

- 1 tsp loose green tea leaves
- 1 cup of water
- honey, lemon, or mint for flavor (optional)

Method

1. Boil water
2. Steep for 2–3 mins and strain.
3. Optional: add lemon or honey. Enjoy!

Tips: Best Times to Drink for Vitality

All types of tea serve their purpose whenever they are consumed. However, taking them at the right time with the right meals can potentially boost their effects. Here are some of the best pairings of different teas, when to take them, and how to benefit from them:

- **Rosemary tea**: Enhance savory meals such as roasted chicken or grilled vegetables with the herbal notes of rosemary tea, perfect for dinner.
- **Matcha tea:** Boost your morning with matcha's vibrant energy. Pair with a light breakfast such as avocado toast or a smoothie.

- **Black tea:** Bold and robust, black tea complements hearty breakfasts. Enjoy it with eggs, bacon, or a classic English breakfast.
- **Ginseng tea**: Invigorate your afternoon slump with ginseng tea. Ideal for a midday pick-me-up, pair it with nuts or fresh fruit.
- **Green tea:** Kick-start your day with green tea's antioxidants. Pair it with a balanced breakfast or enjoy it as a mid-morning refreshment.
- **Ginkgo tea:** Enhance your focus with ginkgo tea. Enjoy it with a light lunch, such as a salad or sushi, to support cognitive function.
- **Yerba mate tea:** Energize your afternoon. Yerba mate pairs well with light snacks such as nuts or a fruit bowl for sustained energy.
- **Sage tea:** Calm your evening with sage tea. It's a great choice with a light dinner or paired with cheese and crackers.
- **Gotu kola chai**: Embrace the soothing properties of gotu kola chai in the evening. Pair it with a light dessert or herbal-infused treats.
- **Pu-erh tea:** Opt for pu-erh tea after a heavy meal. Its earthy tones complement rich dishes, aiding in digestion and providing a satisfying conclusion.

Chapter 10

Seasonal Allergies

E ver find yourself in a battle against the sneezing, itching, and overall discomfort that comes with seasonal allergies? Well, you are not alone. Many people suffer from allergies in one season or another.

Seasonal allergies are the most common and the most frequent illness worldwide. Many people in this world, particularly during the changing of the season from summer to fall and into the early winter season, get allergies. Therefore, these phenomena are called seasonal allergies because they happen due to the changing of the weather.

But fear not! We're about to explore soothing natural remedies in the form of herbal teas to help you conquer these unwelcome guests. These herbal teas will help you embrace each season with open arms.

Allergies Defined and How They Grow into Symptoms

The primary responsibility of the immune system is to make antibodies that protect us from external substances, mostly pollen and other food substances. The immune system makes antibodies to fight against harmful allergens. When the immune system does not make sufficient antibodies, interacting with these allergens can result in inflammation of the skin, airways, and digestive system.

Yet, there is something else that can result in allergies; this one is more scientifically advanced, and only some people might learn about it in school. But trust me, this should answer all of your questions.

Among many immune system functions, one is to make a chemical called allergen-specific immunoglobin, also known as IgE. IgE is an antibody. The purpose of this antibody is to act as an information carrier to the cells with the message that the cells are about to get invaded by foreign particles that the immune system detected as harmful. Therefore, a chemical defense is required, making the cells adapt to protect themselves.

People with allergic reactions often carry high quantities of this IgE chemical. High quantities of IgE cause sneezing, runny nose, itchy eyes, scratchy throat, and other allergic symptoms.

Herbal Teas to Counteract Common Allergens

Before the evolution of Western medicine, for thousands of years, Eastern medicine—particularly herbal teas—dominated as a medicinal treatment for several illnesses including fighting against common allergens. In this section, we will discuss the most useful and effective herbal teas for eradicating allergic symptoms.

Stinging Nettle Tea is a plant with many medicinal properties with due to several anti-inflammatory and antioxidant compounds that significantly reduce symptoms of allergy.

Ginger Tea is also used and considered an herb. Although ginger is a flowering plant, its root serves the purpose of cooking primarily as a spice to add taste. Moreover, there have been reports that show that having ginger tea can also control nasal problems and its symptoms in patients with allergic rhinitis.

Peppermint Tea is your allergy ally! It has natural menthol content that help open up nasal passages, easing congestion and promoting better airflow. This aromatic brew acts as a decongestant, soothing an irritated throat and reducing coughing. Beyond its respiratory benefits, peppermint tea boasts anti-inflammatory properties, alleviating allergy-induced inflammation and making it a perfect antidote to hay fever.

Fennel Tea comes from *Foeniculum* vulgare, a perennial herb of the carrot family. Packed with antioxidants and anti-inflammatory properties, fennel helps calm the storm of allergy symptoms. Its natural compounds may reduce histamine reactions, alleviating sneezing, nasal congestion, and itchy eyes.

Licorice Tea is a great option if nothing works for your allergic symptoms. Licorice could definitely be the cure. Scientifically known as *Glycyrrhiza glabra*, licorice root helps soothe irritated airways and reduce allergy-induced inflammation.

Rose Hips Tea is packed with vitamin C and antioxidants. Research identifies galactolipid as the active ingredient of rose hips tea. These properties will provide relief from pesky symptoms such as nasal congestion and itchy eyes, making it a soothing elixir during allergy seasons.

Chamomile Tea is nature's calming elixir, offering more than bedtime serenity—it's a secret weapon against allergies! Packed with anti-inflammatory properties, chamomile tea takes on the sneezes and sniffles, reducing the intensity of allergic reactions.

Green Tea is a wonderful treatment when it comes to curing allergies and rhinitis. Packed with antioxidants such as catechins, it possesses anti-inflammatory properties that can soothe irritated airways, reducing allergy symptoms.

8 Recipes: Blends to Help Ease the Irritation

Stinging Nettle Tea

Time: 5-10 minutes

Serving Time: Dinner

Prep Time: 2 minutes

Cook Time: 5-10 minutes

Ingredients

- 1 tsp dried stinging nettle leaves
- 1 cup of water
- honey, lemon, or mint for flavor (optional)

Directions

1. Boil the water and add the dried nettle leaves to the water.
2. Reduce the heat to low and let the nettle leaves steep for about 5–10 minutes.
3. If desired, add honey, lemon, or mint to enhance the flavor. Adjust the quantities to suit your taste. It's done!

Ginger Tea

Time: 10–15 minutes

Serving Time: After a meal

Prep Time: 5 minutes

Cook Time: 10–15 minutes

Ingredients

- 1–2 in. of fresh ginger root, peeled and sliced (adjust to taste)
- 1 cup of water
- honey or lemon slices to add taste

Directions

1. Boil your water.
2. Peel the ginger root and cut it into small pieces.
3. Add this to your water.
4. Reduce the heat to low, cover the pot, and let the ginger simmer in the water for about 10–15 minutes.
5. Strain and enjoy!

Peppermint Detox

Time: 7 minutes

Serving Time: Anytime

Prep Time: 2 minutes

Cook Time: 5 minutes

Ingredients

- 1 tbsp dried peppermint leaves
- 1 cup of water
- honey or lemon for added sweetness or flavor (optional)

The Green Glow

Directions

1. Boil a cup of water and then turn off the heat.
2. Add your peppermint leaves and simmer for 5 minutes.
3. Strain the mixture and add the sweetener of your choice.

Fennel-Honey Mix

Time: 7 minutes

Serving Time: Before sleeping

Prep Time: 2 minutes

Cook Time: 5 minutes

Ingredients

- 1 tsp dried fennel seeds
- 1 cup of water
- 1–2 tsp honey (adjust to taste)
- lemon slices for added flavor (optional)

Directions

1. Crush the fennel seeds slightly using a mortar and pestle. If you don't have a mortar and pestle, put the fennel in a plastic bag and crush with the back of a spoon. This helps release the aromatic oils for a richer flavor.
2. Boil 1 cup of water and then turn off the heat.
3. Add the fennel seeds and let them steep in the hot water for about 5–7 minutes.
4. Strain and add honey and that's it!

Licorice Tea

Time: 7 minutes

Serving Time: Anytime

Prep Time: 2 minutes

Cook Time: 5 minutes

Ingredients

- 1 tbsp dried licorice root
- 1 cup of water
- honey or lemon for added sweetness or flavor (optional)

Directions

1. Add your water and licorice root to a pan.
2. Cover the lid and bring it to a boil.
3. Let it simmer on medium heat for 5–7 minutes.
4. Add a little bit of lemon zest for flavor.
5. Remove the tea and strain it into a cup.
6. Add honey for flavor and sip away!

Rose Hip Detox Tea

Time: 10–15 minutes

Serving Time: After breakfast

Prep Time: 2 minutes

Cook Time: 15 minutes

Ingredients

- 1–2 tbsp dried rose hips
- 1 cup of water
- honey as a sweetener
- lemon for flavor

The Green Glow

Directions

1. Boil 1 cups of water.
2. Add your rose hips to the water and turn off the heat.
3. Cover it and let the leaves simmer in water for 10–15 minutes.
4. Strain and add flavors of your choice to make the tea your taste buds desire!

Chamomile Tea

Time: 5 minutes

Serving Time: At night

Prep Time: 2 minutes

Cook Time: 3 minutes

Ingredients

- 1 tsp dried chamomile flowers
- 1 cup of water
- pinch of lemon zest
- honey as a sweetener

Directions

1. Bring 1 cup of water to a boil.
2. Pour in the dried chamomile flowers and turn off the heat.
3. Allow the chamomile to steep in the hot water for about 5 minutes.
4. Flavor it with a pinch of lemon zest and honey according to your taste.
5. Strain and serve.

Green Tea

Time: 5 minutes

Serving Time: Anytime, best after a meal

Prep Time: 2 minutes

Cook Time: 3 minutes

Ingredients

- 1 cup of water
- 1 tsp dried green tea leaves
- lemon juice or sugar/honey for taste

Directions

1. Boil water and then turn off the heat.
2. Add your green tea leaves.
3. Steep for 2–3 minutes, strain, and savor the antioxidant-rich goodness.
4. Add a slice of lemon or a drizzle of honey for an extra delightful touch!

Tips: Combining Teas with Other Holistic Measures

Teas and other herbal mixtures, undoubtedly, play a big role in the treatment of seasonal allergies and flu. However, combining various teas with other holistic measures can create an even more powerful medicine that nurtures not only your mind but also your body and spirit.

Here are some tips you can implement along with teas to muster your quick cures:

- **Proper nutrition:** Teas complement a well-balanced diet, enhancing your nutritional intake. Pair herbal teas with nutrient-rich snacks or meals to create a holistic approach to nourishment. For instance, match a calming lavender tea with a plate of fresh fruits and nuts for a delightful sensory experience.
- **Adequate hydration:** Incorporate herbal teas into your daily hydration routine. Staying well-hydrated is vital for overall health, and herbal infusions contribute to your fluid intake while offering unique health benefits. Hydration, combined with the subtle flavors of herbal teas, supports your body's natural processes.
- **Holistic lifestyle choices:** Teas align seamlessly with other holistic lifestyle choices. Prioritize quality sleep, engage in regular physical activity, and foster meaningful connections. These lifestyle elements, when woven together with your tea rituals, contribute to a holistic approach to wellness.

Remember, holistic well-being is a personal journey. Listen to your body, explore different teas, and embrace practices that resonate with you. The synergy of teas with mindfulness, nutrition, hydration, and lifestyle choices creates a tapestry of wellness—tailored to your unique needs and preferences. So, sip mindfully, breathe deeply, and let the holistic symphony of well-being resonate throughout your life.

Chapter 11

Beyond the Brew—Enhancing Your Tea Experience

So far, we have been your guide on your journey to being a tea expert, finding the perfect tea for every time. However, your journey of transcending the ordinary sip of tea into a special moment still needs a final stop: how to make your tea a personalized, holistic experience.

In this chapter we are about to give you some tips to enhance your tea experience, where each cup becomes a special moment that you hold close to your heart.

Tea, with its roots steeped in ancient traditions, has long been celebrated for its ability to comfort, revive, and heal. But what if we told you there's more to your teacup than meets the eye? What if, beyond the warmth and flavor, lies a realm where herbs and intention intertwine to create an elixir that not only delights your taste buds but nurtures your body, mind, and spirit? All this happens with the enriching phenomena of added sweeteners and taste enhancers!

This chapter is all about the art of enhancing your tea experience.

Let's explore healthy alternatives to refined sugar and learn modern brewing techniques.

Natural Herbal Sweeteners

Teas have their superpowers. However, sweeteners and sugar enhance their flavors in unexpected ways. The most commonly used sweetener is refined, granulated sugar. This is where we need to push a pause and re-evaluate our choices.

On one hand, we are looking forward to improving our health with various herbal drinks, but refined sugar negates the benefits. Impaired blood sugar regulation, over time, can lead to chronic health problems like diabetes. Ask yourself, "Do I want that to happen?" No, right?!

So, if you're looking to sweeten the deal without compromising on health, natural herbal sweeteners are your go-to pals. To make things easier for you, we have compiled a few alternatives that you can use to sweeten your tea instead of the usual refined options.

Allulose

Allulose is a rare sugar found naturally in small quantities in some fruits and sweeteners like maple syrup. The cool thing about allulose is that it looks and tastes like sugar, but here's the kicker: It's almost calorie-free! It has only 0.2 calories per gram! Yep you heard that right. So, if you're watching your waistline or just trying to make smarter choices, allulose is a sweet deal.

Unlike regular sugar, allulose won't send your blood sugar levels on a rollercoaster ride. It has a low glycemic index, which means it won't cause those energy-crashes after your tea break.

However, with allulose, moderation is key. Just because allulose is a healthier alternative doesn't mean you should drown your tea in sweetness. Taking too much allulose can also lead to diarrhea, bloating, and abdominal pain.

Honey

When going healthy with sugars, honey is the first thing that comes to our mind—and rightfully so. It is one of the natural sweeteners produced by nature that can be consumed without any further processing, as bees have already done that job for you. It contains various antioxidants, enzymes, and minerals that can contribute to your overall well-being.

Maple Syrup

Maple syrup is one of the hidden gems of the herbal world. Some would call it liquid gold. Made from the saps of the maple tree, this syrup adds a rich, caramelized flavor to your cup. Given its rich sugary taste, many might think, *Isn't maple syrup just sugar in disguise?* Trust us, it's not! While it does contain sugar, it also boasts a lower glycemic index compared to plain old white sugar. Moreover, its rich choice of antioxidants and minerals also gives your body an extra health boost with every cup, making it an excellent choice of herbal sweetener!

Sugar Alcohol

Sugar alcohol, such as xylitol or erythritol, can be another great herbal alternative to refined sugars for your tea. An interesting fact; sugar alcohols don't promote tooth decay. This is because the bacteria in your mouth cannot process these sugar alcohols, protecting your teeth from decay. So, say goodbye to worrying about cavities when you sip your herbal brew. All of that being said, you still need to be cautious with your intake because consumption of too much sugar alcohol can lead to diarrhea. We don't see sugar alcohol as the best alternative sweetener, but it still makes the list as a viable option.

Monk Fruit

Lo han guo, also known as monk fruit juice, is often dubbed the "longevity fruit." It is a stellar choice for those seeking a healthier alternative to refined sugar in their herbal teas. The juice is extracted from the *Siraitia grosvenorii* fruit, which is native to southern China. This natural sweetener boasts zero calories and is 100–250 times sweeter than sugar. Unlike regular sugar, monk juice doesn't cause blood sugar spikes, making it diabetic-friendly. It's a delightful way to sweeten your tea without compromising on flavor or health-conscious choices.

Palmyra Blossom

Palmyra blossom emerges as a delightful and nutritious alternative to refined sugar, adding a touch of sweetness to your herbal teas. Extracted from the blossoms of the palmyra palm tree, this natural sweetener not only enhances flavor but also brings along a host of health benefits. Palmyra is rich in vitamins and minerals, especially vitamin B12. Palmyra blossom also boasts a lower glycemic index (GI), 40 to be precise. In comparison, regular sugar has a GI of 100. Thus, palmyra is a wise choice for those mindful of their blood sugar levels.

Organic Coconut Sugar

Organic coconut sugar is a sweet revelation for herbal tea lovers looking to ditch refined sugar. It is packed with essential minerals such as potassium, iron, and zinc. It not only sweetens your tea but also offers a nutritional boost. Coconut sugar has a low glycemic index means a steadier energy release, preventing sugar crashes. However, with 39% of fructose levels, coconut sugar does have its downside. Therefore, always use it carefully.

Date Sugar

Although it might feel out of context, date sugar is yet another natural alternative to refined sugar when sweetening your herbal tea. Made from dried and ground dates, it retains the fruit's nutrients, such as fiber, potassium, and antioxidants. Just like other herbal sweeteners, date sugar also has a low GI.

Tips and Tricks for Brewing

Brewing can be a fun-filled task. However, if you mess up this step, instead of getting a healing cup of tea, you can end up with a disaster on your hands. To avoid this altogether, we have compiled a list of tips and tricks from around the world to make your tea-making a wholesome experience.

Let's dig in to find out what tricks you need to get a great cup of tea that leaves an amazing aftertaste:

- **Perfect temperature is key:** To level up your game, experiment with water temperature; black teas love a hot bath, while green teas prefer a gentler soak. This can help you to extract unique flavors. Play the temperature tango —a little hotter for a bolder taste and a little cooler for a smoother profile.
- **Experiment with flavor fusions:** Get creative with your ingredients! Mix and match flavors that you wouldn't normally associate with your brew. Try adding a hint of cinnamon to your coffee or a sprig of mint to your tea. Who knows? You might discover a new favorite combination.
- **Understand the power of timing:** Timing the brewing is one of the main steps of tea-making. Timing it a little too short may give you incomplete blends, while too much time can destroy the flavors altogether. On the other hand, some

herbal teas take a bit longer for a robust taste but keep a close eye on delicate green teas to avoid bitterness. And if you're feeling fancy, try cold brewing for a refreshing twist.

- **Try infused aromatherapy brews:** Infuse aromatherapy into your brewing routine by incorporating fragrant herbs or essential oils. Lavender-infused coffee or chamomile-infused tea, anyone? It's a delightful way to engage your senses.
- **Use mood lighting:** Set the mood with ambient lighting. Brew under the warm glow of string lights or candlelight. It creates a cozy atmosphere and adds a touch of romance to your brewing routine.

Remember, brewing is not only a science; it's also an art. Put on your creative hat, dance a little, and let the brewing adventure begin. Cheers to your next delicious concoction!

Tea Additives That Enhance Your Flavors

Tea-making is all about flavors and experimenting with these flavors is what makes it much more exciting. In this pursuit, additives are one more additional element that makes tea heaven for our tastebuds.

There is a whole range of additives that you can use to make your teas more tempting. Fresh herbs such as mint or basil impart a refreshing twist, while a dash of citrusy zest from lemon or orange peel adds zing.

The exciting part is you can also experiment with spices! Cinnamon or ginger can lend warmth, and a hint of cardamom brings exotic notes. For a sweet touch, honey or agave syrup harmonizes beautifully. Don't forget edible flowers such as chamomile or lavender for a fragrant infusion.

Modern Tea Practices

The modern-day practices of tea-making are different from the ancient times. In modern tea practices, the focus has shifted from ritual to routine. Artisanal blends, eco-friendly packaging, and sustainable sourcing have taken center stage. Moreover, the brewing is done in infusers and tea gadgets that ensure the precision and convenience of taste blending.

Cold brewing and tea mixology have redefined how we enjoy our favorite leafy beverage, introducing refreshing iced teas and tea-based cocktails. With modern methods, sustainability is paramount focusing on eco-friendly packaging and ethical sourcing.

Social media platforms also foster tea communities, sharing experiences and discoveries and spreading the goodness of herbal teas to more and more people. In a nutshell, modern tea culture encapsulates a dynamic fusion of ancient rituals, contemporary creativity, and a global passion for this timeless elixir.

Ethical and Sustainable Tea Consumption

Like all other industries, the tea industry has gone through renovation. The sustainable shift in the past few decades has turned and improved tea making and consumption in many ways.

Ethical and sustainable tea consumption is a conscientious approach that considers the social and environmental impact of tea production. It involves the following approaches:

- supporting fair-trade practices
- ensuring fair wages and humane working conditions for tea workers
- supporting sustainable farming methods, such as organic

> cultivation and biodiversity preservation, to reduce the ecological footprint of tea production
>
> - choosing teas with transparent sourcing practices, emphasizing ethical labor and eco-friendly processes
> - opting for reusable tea accessories, as they minimize single-use packaging and ultimately pollution

Ethical tea consumption is about embracing a commitment to the well-being of communities and the planet. This practice goes beyond the cup—it's about supporting communities, respecting nature, and sipping with a conscience. So, let your tea ritual be a mindful journey, where every sip tells a story of sustainability, ethical sourcing, and a commitment to a better, greener world.

Bonus Chapter: Holiday Themed Recipes

No matter what winter holiday you celebrate, you can embrace the comfort and warming properties of aromatic herbs. The dark and cold months of winter inspire our desire to warm our bones and find a light in the long, dark days. How can we find comfort and pleasure in herbal teas to lift our spirits?

Sharing herbal teas that evoke the holiday spirit with our friends and loved ones further enhances the holiday spirit, creating sweet memories for us to cherish and reflect on. What can be more comforting than the aroma of cinnamon, star anise, ginger, or nutmeg delighting your senses next to a cracking fire, perhaps with a good book?

Immerse yourself in the world of festive herbal tea blends to try out this holiday season with the following recipes.

Autumn Harvest Spice

Time: 20 minutes

Serving Time: Evening

Prep Time: 5 minutes

Cook Time: 15 minutes

Ingredients

- a couple of fresh apple slices
- 1 cinnamon stick
- sprinkle of dried orange peel
- 1 clove
- 1 cup of water
- a couple of slices of fresh ginger root

Directions

1. Combine apple slices, cinnamon sticks, dried orange peel, cloves, and ginger root in boiling water.
2. Simmer for 15 minutes, then strain and serve.

Cranberry Citrus Zest

Time: 18 minutes

Serving Time: Afternoon

Prep Time: 3 minutes

Cook Time: 15 minutes

Ingredients

- 1/2 tsp dried cranberries
- dash of lemon zest
- dash of orange zest
- 1/2 tsp dried hibiscus flowers
- 1/2 tsp dried rose hips

- 1 cup of water

Directions

1. Add cranberries, lemon zest, orange zest, hibiscus, and rose hips to hot water.
2. Steep for 15 minutes.
3. Strain, and enjoy.

Pumpkin Pie Delight

Time: 25 minutes

Serving Time: Morning

Prep Time: 10 minutes

Cook Time: 15 minutes

Ingredients

- 1 tsp pumpkin puree
- 1 cup of milk
- 1 cinnamon stick
- dash of nutmeg
- 1 clove
- drop of vanilla extract

Directions

1. Mix pumpkin puree with cinnamon sticks, nutmeg, cloves, and a split vanilla bean in milk.
2. Simmer for 15 minutes. Do not allow the milk to boil.
3. Strain, and serve warm.

Maple Cinnamon Toast

Time: 20 minutes

Serving Time: Evening

Prep Time: 5 minutes

Cook Time: 15 minutes

Ingredients

- 1 tsp loose rooibos tea
- 1 cinnamon stick
- maple syrup, to taste
- pinch of dried orange peel
- 1 cup of water

Directions

1. Brew rooibos tea with cinnamon sticks and orange peel.
2. Simmer for 15 minutes.
3. Add maple syrup to taste, strain, and serve.

Spiced Apple Chai

Time: 15 minutes

Serving Time: Afternoon

Prep Time: 5 minutes

Cook Time: 10 minutes

Ingredients

- 1 tsp black tea leaves
- a couple of slices of fresh apple
- 1 cinnamon stick

The Green Glow

- 1 cardamom pod, crushed
- 1 clove
- 1 cup of water

Directions

1. Combine black tea leaves, diced apples, cinnamon, cardamom, and cloves in freshly boiled water.
2. Simmer for 10 minutes, strain, and enjoy.

Nutty Vanilla Rooibos

Time: 20 minutes

Serving Time: Afternoon

Prep Time: 5 minutes

Cook Time: 15 minutes

Ingredients

- 1 tsp loose rooibos tea
- a drop of almond extract
- a drop of vanilla bean extract
- a dash of cinnamon
- 1 cup of water

Directions

1. Brew rooibos tea with almond extract, vanilla bean extract, and cinnamon.
2. Simmer for 15 minutes.
3. Strain and enjoy.

Cozy Clove Citrus

Time: 12 minutes

Serving Time: Morning

Prep Time: 2 minutes

Cook Time: 10 minutes

Ingredients

- 1 clove
- dash of dried orange peel
- dash of lemon zest
- 1 tsp black tea leaves
- 1 cup of water
- honey, to taste (optional)

Directions

1. Boil cloves, orange peel, and lemon zest for 20 minutes.
2. Add black tea, steep for 10 minutes.
3. Strain, sweeten with honey if desired, and serve.

Harvest Moon Mint

Time: 15 minutes

Serving Time: Night

Prep Time: 5 minutes

Cook Time: 10 minutes

Ingredients

- 1 tsp dried peppermint leaves
- 1 tsp dried chamomile flowers

The Green Glow

- ½ tsp dried lavender buds
- dash of lemon zest
- 1 cup of water

Directions

1. Combine peppermint leaves, chamomile, lavender, and lemon zest in freshly boiled water.
2. Steep for 10 minutes, strain, and enjoy a relaxing cup.

Winter Berry Bliss

Time: 15 minutes

Serving Time: Evening

Prep Time: 5 minutes

Cook Time: 10 minutes

Ingredients

- 1 tsp hibiscus petals
- ½ tsp dried elderberries
- 1 cinnamon stick
- dash of dried orange peel
- 1 star anise
- 1 cup of water

Directions

1. Simmer hibiscus petals, elderberries, cinnamon, orange peel, and star anise in freshly boiled water for 10 minutes.
2. Strain and enjoy.

Gingerbread Warmth

Time: 18 minutes

Serving Time: Morning

Prep Time: 3 minutes

Cook Time: 15 minutes

Ingredients

- a couple of fresh ginger slices
- 1 cinnamon stick
- ½ tsp allspice berries
- a drop of vanilla extract
- 1 tsp black tea leaves
- 1 cup of water

Directions

1. Add ginger, cinnamon, allspice, and vanilla bean in freshly boiled water and simmer for 15 minutes.
2. Add black tea and steep for 3 minutes.
3. Strain and serve.

Cozy Apple Cinnamon

Time: 28 minutes

Serving Time: Evening

Prep Time: 10 minutes

Cook Time: 18 minutes

Ingredients

- a couple of dried apple slices

The Green Glow

- 1 cinnamon sticks
- 1 clove
- dash of nutmeg
- 1 tsp loose rooibos tea
- 1 cup of water

Directions

1. Combine apple slices, cinnamon, clove, and nutmeg in freshly boiled water. Simmer for 15 minutes.
2. Add rooibos tea and simmer for 3 miniutes.
3. Strain and enjoy.

Festive Cranberry Orange

Time: 20 minutes

Serving Time: Afternoon

Prep Time: 5 minutes

Cook Time: 15 minutes

Ingredients

- ½ tsp dried cranberries
- dash of dried orange peel
- ½ tsp rose hips
- ½ tsp hibiscus petals
- dash of cinnamon
- 1 cup of water

Directions

1. Steep cranberries, orange peel, rose hips, hibiscus, and cinnamon in freshly boiled water for 15 minutes.

2. Strain and serve.

Spiced Vanilla Chai

Time: 15 minutes

Serving Time: Morning

Prep Time: 5 minutes

Cook Time: 10minutes

Ingredients

- 1 tsp black tea leaves
- 1 cinnamon stick
- 1 cardamom pod, crushed
- 1 clove
- a couple of fresh ginger slices
- a drop of vanilla extract
- 1 cup of water
- splash of milk

Directions

1. Simmer black tea, cinnamon, cardamom, cloves, ginger, and vanilla in water for 15 minutes.
2. Add milk if desired.
3. Strain and serve.

Wintergreen Wonderland

Time: 15 minutes

Serving Time: Evening

Prep Time: 5 minutes

The Green Glow

Cook Time: 10 minutes

Ingredients

- 1/2 tsp dried wintergreen leaves
- 1/2 tsp spearmint leaves
- ½ tsp lemon balm
- 1 cup of water

Directions

1. Steep wintergreen, spearmint, and lemon balm in hot water for 10 minutes.
2. Strain and enjoy.

Yuletide Citrus Spice

Time: 22 minutes

Serving Time: Afternoon

Prep Time: 2 minutes

Cook Time: 20 minutes

Ingredients

- dash of orange peel
- dash of lemon zest
- a couple of fresh ginger slices
- 1 star anise
- 1 tsp black tea leaves
- 1 cup of water

Directions

1. Boil orange peel, lemon zest, ginger, and star anise for 20 minutes.
2. Add black tea, steep for 2 minutes.
3. Strain and enjoy.

Snowy Night Mint

Time: 20 minutes

Serving Time: Night

Prep Time: 5 minutes

Cook Time: 15 minutes

Ingredients

- ½ tsp Peppermint leaves
- 1 tsp White tea leaves
- ½ tsp dried blueberries
- ¼ tsp lavender buds
- 1 cup of water

Directions

1. Simmer peppermint, white tea, blueberries, and lavender in freshly boiled water 15 minutes.
2. Strain and enjoy a soothing cup.

Midnight Berry Sparkle

Time: 20 minutes

Serving Time: Midnight

Prep Time: 5 minutes

The Green Glow

Cook Time: 15 minutes

Ingredients

- ½ tsp dried blackberries
- ½ tsp dried raspberries
- 1 tsp hibiscus petals
- ½ tsp fresh mint leaves
- 1 cup of water
- Honey (optional)

Directions

1. Steep blackberries, raspberries, hibiscus petals, and mint leaves in boiling water. Turn off the heat and steep for 15 minutes.
2. Strain, sweeten with honey if desired, and serve.

New Year Citrus Cleanse

Time: 18 minutes

Serving Time: Morning

Prep Time: 3 minutes

Cook Time: 15 minutes

Ingredients

- dash of lemon zest
- dash of orange zest
- 1 tsp green tea leaves
- a couple of ginger slices
- 1 cup of water

Directions

1. Simmer lemon zest, orange zest, and ginger slices in water for 15 minutes.
2. Add green tea leaves, steep for 3 minutes.
3. Strain and enjoy.

Celebration Chamomile Delight

Time: 15 minutes

Serving Time: Evening

Prep Time: 5 minutes

Cook Time: 10 minutes

Ingredients

- 1 tsp chamomile flowers
- ¼ tsp lavender buds
- 1 tsp rose petals
- drop of vanilla extract
- 1 cup of water

Directions

1. Infuse chamomile, lavender, rose petals, and vanilla extract in freshly boiled water for 10 minutes.
2. Strain and serve.

Fresh Start Peppermint

Time: 13 minutes

Serving Time: Morning

Prep Time: 5 minutes

The Green Glow

Cook Time: 8 minutes

Ingredients

- 1/2 tsp peppermint leaves
- ½ tsp lemon balm
- 1 tsp green tea leaves
- honey, to taste (optional)
- 1 cup of water

Directions

1. Steep peppermint leaves and lemon balm in freshly boiled water for 5 minutes on a low simmer.
2. Add in green tea and steep for 3 minutes.
3. Strain, add honey to taste, and enjoy.

New Horizons Hibiscus

Time: 25 minutes

Serving Time: Afternoon

Prep Time: 10 minutes

Cook Time: 15 minutes

Ingredients

- 1 tsp hibiscus petals
- 1 cinnamon stick
- dash of orange peel
- 1 star anise
- 1 cup of water

Directions

1. Simmer hibiscus petals, cinnamon sticks, orange peel, and star anise in freshly boiled water for 15 minutes.
2. Strain and serve.

First Dawn Fruit Medley

Time: 18 minutes

Serving Time: Morning

Prep Time: 3 minutes

Cook Time: 15 minutes

Ingredients

- a couple of dried apple slices
- a couple of dried apricots
- 1 cinnamon stick
- 1 tsp dried rose hips

Directions

1. Combine dried apple slices, apricots, cinnamon sticks, and rose hips in hot water.
2. Steep for 15 minutes, strain, and savor.

Winter Warmer Vanilla

Time: 20 minutes

Serving Time: Evening

Prep Time: 5 minutes

Cook Time: 15 minutes

The Green Glow

- a drop of vanilla extract
- 1 tsp loose rooibos tea
- 1 cinnamon stick
- a dash of nutmeg
- 1 cup of water

Directions

1. Brew rooibos tea with vanilla extract, cinnamon, and nutmeg.
2. Simmer for 15 minutes, strain, and enjoy.

Serene Star Anise Elixir

Time: 15 minutes

Serving Time: Night

Prep Time: 5 minutes

Cook Time: 10 minutes

Ingredients

- 1 star anise
- ¼ tsp fennel seeds
- ½ tsp licorice root
- 1 tsp lemon balm
- 1 cup of water

Directions

1. Combine star anise, fennel seeds, licorice root, and lemon balm in hot water.
2. Steep for 10 minutes, strain, and enjoy a soothing cup.

Conclusion

Herbal teas are delicious. But there's more to herbal teas beyond the delightful taste. Much more. Herbal teas infuse your body with the healing qualities of herbs. All of the properties that have been mentioned through this guide make herbal teas a popular choice among many. All over the world, people have been using herbal teas for a long time and, clearly, for a good reason.

Here is a quick recap of how herbal teas are super beneficial to incorporate into your day-to-day routine:

Revisiting the Benefits of Herbal Teas

Your Answer to Burnout

Herbal teas are refreshing for your nervous system and mental health. If you are someone who relies on caffeinated drinks to refresh during burnout, herbal tea can help. Botanicals can bring down your stress levels—no matter what stage of burnout you are in.

Special Mention: Chamomile Tea

Beat the Bloat

Herbal tea is a best friend of the digestive system. Herbs make sure that your digestive flow is fully functional and working. Hence, using teas can help relax the muscles of your gastrointestinal tract, reducing the feeling of discomfort. Overall, they promote a sense of digestive ease.

Special Mention: Peppermint Tea, Dandelion Tea

Say Goodbye to Chronic Diseases

We cannot understate the healing properties of herbal teas. For individuals suffering from chronic diseases, herbs can serve as an anti-inflammatory, antioxidant, and calming medicine.

Herbs are widely used to balance blood sugar levels and keep your heart healthy. In return, you may develop protection against chronic diseases like diabetes, cancer, and stroke.

Important: *If you are suffering from a chronic disease, please consult with your healthcare professional before incorporating any herbal tea into your diet. They will provide you with personalized guidance and treatment plans.*

Special Mention: Rooibos Tea, Hibiscus Tea

Flu and Cold, No More

Herbs carry antioxidants, vitamins, minerals, and polyphenols. All of these are your golden ticket to stay healthy during the cold and flu season.

A variety of herbal teas have anti-inflammatory and immune enhancing properties to reduce the effects of sore throat. Moreover, the mint teas contain a special element called menthol that promotes easier breathing through a stuffy nose.

Special Mention: Ginger Tea, Peppermint Tea

Look Young and Healthy

Let's accept it: We all want to look younger than we are. While there is nothing we can do about the passing of time, we can reduce the physical signs of aging—all thanks to herbal teas.

Many herbal teas carry antioxidants that fight free radicals. Free radicals are the chemicals causing oxidative damage to our skin. Free radicals lead to loss of elasticity and the appearance of wrinkles on the skin. To combat those premature aging factors, a simply enjoy a cup of tea regularly.

Special Mention: Hibiscus Tea

Concentrate Better

Clear the brain fog with a warm cup of herbal tea. Herbal teas are good to start your day when you require focus and concentration. Herbal teas can encourage blood to flow straight to your brain, giving your brain the oxygen boost it needs to connect to the task at hand better.

In fact, some herbal teas are also known to improve brain function and prevent brain diseases such as Alzheimer's and Parkinson's.

Special Mention: Ginkgo

Herbal Teas are the Future of Wellness and Cuisine

With plenty of benefits, one thing is for sure: Herbal teas are the future of wellness and cuisine. Reports state that the herbal tea market is set to increase from USD 3.47 billion (2022) to USD 4.88 billion (2030). The annual growth rate of herbal teas will be 5% over the forecast period of 2022 to 2030.

Herbal teas have caught the attention of individuals throughout the world because of two main reasons: the delightful flavors and the unlimited health benefits. Consumers today are very conscious about their health, thus the herbal tea market has turned into a thriving business.

What Is the Market Potential?

Wellness

With time, consumers are becoming aware of the health advantages of herbal teas. These drinks are typically made from different herbs, spices, flowers, and fruits and serve as a great alternative to regular tea and coffee.

Getting a great flavor along with a wide range of medical benefits is like a win-win situation. As people continue to search for drinks that support wellness, the demand for herbal tea is surging.

Cuisine

Apart from the health factor, the herbal tea market is well-known for its variety of flavors and blends that cater to the taste preferences of all types of consumers. Some new additions such as turmeric and hibiscus are rapidly becoming everyone's favorite. However, the old blends such as peppermint, ginger, and chamomile are no less popular.

Many producers are happy to experiment with uncommon blends. Exotic components such as lemongrass, turmeric, and pu'erh have been introduced to herbal teas. This wide variety helps individuals to customize their tea as per their preferences.

What Is Driving the Growth?

The growth in the herbal tea market is dependent on many factors. Several variables include increasing consumer demand, technological advancements, and a constant shift in consumer preferences.

Growing consumer awareness stands out. There is an increased consciousness in the market created by consumers who want healthier, and more natural alternatives.

Moreover, the advancements in the technological sector are also somewhat responsible for the growing popularity of herbal teas. Today, more efficient and sustainable production methods are being used in the production of these teas.

Keep Exploring

Our exploration of the world of herbal tea is coming to an end. However, we urge you to take it from here and keep exploring.

It is on you to:

Mix Your Own Tea

You can become your own tea artist! Mix different plants to make your own special tea. Maybe try lavender with peppermint or chamomile with lemongrass. The sky is the limit. Have fun as you create your unique tea blends.

Cook With Tea

Tea is not just for drinking. You can use it in cooking, too. Try putting tea in your food, such as desserts and sauces. For example, matcha is trendy in desserts and smoothies. is like going on a tasteful adventure in your kitchen. Be creative with how you use it.

Share With Friends

Sharing and exploring herbal tea with your friends can be fun. Join our Facebook group Herbs, Hearts, and Healing and let's start trying new teas together.

Our group is dedicated to herbal enthusiasts and curious souls. It caters to all—whether you are just starting your herbal journey or have years of experience in the field. Join our community to learn, share, and grow together.

We have dedicated the space to those who want to participate in vibrant discussions about herbs, share herbal creations, and/or seek advice from fellow plant lovers. Some of the core objectives of our group are to create a community with respect, inclusivity, and a shared passion for the pharmacy of nature.

With your help, we aim to create a group where everyone's voice is heard and unique knowledge is shared. Our collective passion for herbs unites us.

However, it is important that you consult your healthcare professionals before making any serious medical changes in your diet. While we all celebrate the knowledge within the community together, every individual is unique and has different circumstances.

An Exciting End to an Exciting Journey

Herbal teas are magical, and it is evident that these magical drinks have so much to offer. Be it their spicy taste, wonderful aroma, or numerous health benefits, they can be a good addition to your routine.

From promoting mental well-being to physical fitness, herbal teas are continuously earning their place as a beloved drink throughout the world. So, whenever you are on the lookout for a morning special energy boost or an evening wind-down ritual, a warm cup of herbal tea or a refreshing iced tea will keep you hooked.

There is an herbal tea for every palate. And, to figure out which one works the best for you, get help from **The Green Glow.** With us, you can make tea time a moment of self-care and joy. And if you found this guide helpful, we graciously ask that you please leave us a review on Amazon.

Conclusion

We're glad that you were a part of our herbal tea story. We hope that you continue to cherish the proven remedies that lie within herbal teas. May the beneficial properties of these drinks continue to make your daily life fulfilling. Here's to a lifetime of well-being, health, and serenity. Sip healthy!

Thanks For Reading!

Hey! Thanks for taking the time to read this and may the seeds of knowledge we've planted grow and flourish. One last thing, and at this point we probably sound like a broken record, but it would mean a great deal to us if you left a review. Also, don't forget to grab your freebie if you haven't already! Just scan the code. See you in the Facebook group!

Yes, I almost forgot my freebie

Bibliography

Allergies - symptoms and causes. (2018). Mayo Clinic. https://www.mayoclinic. org/diseases-conditions/allergies/symptoms-causes/syc-20351497

Antigen: What it is, function, types, & testing. (2022, August 16). Cleveland Clinic. https://my.clevelandclinic.org/health/diseases/24067-antigen

Best drinks for enlarged prostate (BPH): green tea and more. (2021, November 2). Healthline. https://www.healthline.com/health/enlarged-prostate/green-tea-bph

Bobiș, O., et al (2018). Honey and diabetes: The importance of natural simple sugars in diet for preventing and treating different types of diabetes. *Oxidative Medicine and Cellular Longevity, 2018,* 1–12. https://doi.org/10.1155/2018/4757893

Chang, G., et al. (2022). Nasal irrigation with licorice extract (Glycyrrhiza glabra) in treating nasal polyps by reducing fibroblast differentiation and extracellular matrix production in TGF-β1-stimulated nasal polyp-derived fibroblasts by inhibiting the MAPK/ERK-1/2 pathway – an in vitro and in clinic study. *BMC Complementary Medicine and Therapies, 22*(1). https://doi.org/10.1186/s12906-022-03791-y

Chen, X., et al. (2015). Efficacy and safety of extract of Ginkgo biloba as an adjunct therapy in chronic schizophrenia: A systematic review of randomized, double-blind, placebo-controlled studies with meta-analysis. *Psychiatry Research, 228*(1), 121–127. https://doi.org/10.1016/j.psychres.2015.04.026

Choe, J. (2020, February 25). *Yerba mate tea health benefits and how to make properly.* Oh, How Civilized. https://www.ohhowcivilized.com/yerba-mate/#Steps_to_Make_Hot_Yerba_Mate_Tea

Cohen, M. (2012). Rosehip - An evidence-based herbal medicine for inflammation and arthritis. *Australian Family Physician, 41*(7), 495–498. https://pubmed.ncbi.nlm.nih.gov/22762068

Disosa, D. (2023, September 13). *Herbal tea market.* https://www.linkedin.com/posts/daniel-disosa-4ab4a4239_%3F%3F%3F%3F%3F%3F-%3F%3F%3F-%3F%3F%3F%3F%3F-%3F%3F%3F-activity-7107534694912540672-8Wjg

Effect of curcuminoids on oxidative stress: A systematic review and meta-analysis of randomized controlled trials. (2015). *Journal of Functional Foods, 18,* 898–909. https://doi.org/10.1016/j.jff.2015.01.005

Energy metabolism - an overview. (n.d.) ScienceDirect Topics. https://www.

sciencedirect.com/topics/agricultural-and-biological-sciences/energy-metabolism

8 herbal tea recipes to boost your immune system. (2020, May 20). Condé Nast Traveler India. https://www.cntraveller.in/story/8-herbal-tea-recipes-to-boost-your-immune-system-turmeric-haldi-ginger-tulsi

Felman, A. (2020, September 7). *Pain: What it is and how to treat it.* https://www.medicalnewstoday.com/articles/145750

15 quick and easy tea recipes for better sleep. (2016, March 9). The Sleep Judge. https://www.thesleepjudge.com/tea-recipes-better-sleep

5 herbal teas that can do wonders for skin and hair health. (n.d.) NDTV Food. https://food.ndtv.com/beauty/5-herbal-teas-that-can-do-wonders-for-skin-and-hair-health-3092866

5 teas that will make your skin glow. (2016, July 17). Mind Body Green. https://www.mindbodygreen.com/articles/teas-for-glowing-skin

5 teas you should drink and avoid on your period. (2019, March 16). Afternoon Tea Reads. https://afternoonteareads.com/5-teas-you-should-drink-and-avoid-on-your-period

5 ways to keep your digestive system healthy. (2019, April 26). Doctor On Demand. https://doctorondemand.com/blog/health/5-ways-to-keep-your-digestive-system-healthy

Franchi, F., et al. (2021). Effects of D-allulose on glucose tolerance and insulin response to a standard oral sucrose load: results of a prospective, randomized, crossover study. *BMJ Open Diabetes Research and Care*, *9*(1), e001939. https://doi.org/10.1136/bmjdrc-2020-001939

Garner-Wizard, M., et al. (2020). HerbClip. *Am J Otolaryngol*, *42*(1), 102743. https://doi.org/10.1016/j.amjoto.2020.102743

Ginkgo biloba tea recipe. (n.d.) Martha Stewart. https://www.marthastewart.com/1049727/ginkgo-biloba-tea

Hay fever - Symptoms and causes. (2019). Mayo Clinic. https://www.mayoclinic.org/diseases-conditions/hay-fever/symptoms-causes/syc-20373039

Herbs for sleep - 6 herbs to improve your sleep. (2021, June 28). Nectar sleep. https://www.nectarsleep.com/posts/herbs-for-sleep

How to brew herbal tea: temperature, steeping Tips, etc. (2019, December 16). Simple Loose Leaf Tea Company. https://simplelooseleaf.com/blog/herbal-tea/how-to-brew-herbal-tea

How to make tea taste better: 9 natural ingredients to add. (3 March, 2023). Seven Teas. https://seventeas.com/how-to-make-tea-taste-better-9-natural-ingredients-to-add

Hudson, J. B. (2011). Applications of the phytomedicine echinacea purpurea (purple coneflower) in infectious diseases. *Journal of Biomedicine and Biotechnology*, 2012, 1–16. https://doi.org/10.1155/2012/769896

Inoue, T., et al. (2001). Effects of peppermint (Mentha piperita L.) extracts on experimental allergic rhinitis in rats. *Biological & Pharmaceutical Bulletin, 24*(1), 92–95. https://doi.org/10.1248/bpb.24.92

Isbill, J., et al. (2020). Opportunities for health promotion: Highlighting herbs and spices to improve immune support and well-being. *Integrative Medicine (Encinitas, Calif.), 19*(5), 30–42. https://www.ncbi.nlm.nih.gov/pmc/articles/PMC7815254

Janeway, C. A., et al. (2001). Immunological memory. *Immunobiology: The Immune System in Health and Disease. 5th Edition.* https://www.ncbi.nlm.nih.gov/books/NBK27158

Jia, W., et al. (2022). Pu-erh tea: A review of a healthful brew. *Journal of Traditional Chinese Medical Sciences.* https://doi.org/10.1016/j.jtcms.2022.04.005

Jiang, S., et al. (2020). Review on d-allulose: In vivo metabolism, catalytic mechanism, engineering strain construction, bio-production technology. *Frontiers in Bioengineering and Biotechnology, 8.* https://doi.org/10.3389/fbioe.2020.00026

Kamei, A., et al. (2022). Development of mouse model for oral allergy syndrome to identify IgE cross-reactive pollen and food allergens: ragweed pollen cross-reacts with fennel and black pepper. *Frontiers in Immunology, 13.* https://doi.org/10.3389/fimmu.2022.945222

Lilly, C. (2023, February 21). *Best digestive tea recipe.* Good Food Baddie, https://goodfoodbaddie.com/best-digestive-tea-recipe

Lin, L. (2022, January 19). *How to make ginseng tea.* Healthy Nibbles by Lisa Lin. https://healthynibblesandbits.com/how-to-make-ginseng-tea

Maeda-Yamamoto, M., et al. (2009). The efficacy of early treatment of seasonal allergic rhinitis with benifuuki green tea containing O-methylated catechin before pollen exposure: an open randomized study. *Allergology International: Official Journal of the Japanese Society of Allergology, 58*(3), 437–444. https://doi.org/10.2332/allergolint.08-OA-0066

McCarty, M. F., et al. (2015). Capsaicin may have important potential for promoting vascular and metabolic health: Table 1. *Open Heart, 2*(1), e000262. https://doi.org/10.1136/openhrt-2015-000262

Mashhadi, N. S., et al. (2013). Anti-oxidative and anti-inflammatory effects of ginger in health and physical activity: review of current evidence. *International Journal of Preventive Medicine, 4*(Suppl 1), S36-42. https://www.ncbi.nlm.nih.gov/pmc/articles/PMC3665023

Matcha 101 - What it is and how to use it recipe. (2020, April 17). Love and Lemons. https://www.loveandlemons.com/matcha-green-tea

National Institute of allergy and infectious diseases. (n.d.) NIAID. http://www.niaid.nih.gov

9 herbal teas that are good for skin and hair. (2016, January 22). The Times of India. https://timesofindia.indiatimes.com/life-style/beauty/9-herbal-teas-that-are-good-for-skin-and-hair/articleshow/47329526.cms

Orhan, I. E. (2012). Centella asiatica (L.) urban: From traditional medicine to modern medicine with neuroprotective potential. *Evidence-Based Complementary and Alternative Medicine, 2012,* 1–8. https://doi.org/10.1155/2012/946259

Overhiser, S. (2020, June 6). *Rosemary tea.* A Couple Cooks. https://www.acouplecooks.com/rosemary-tea

Phoenix, S. (2023, July 21). *10 top herbs that boost testosterone levels.* Great Green Wall. https://www.greatgreenwall.org/supplements/herbs-boost-testosterone

Powell, J. (2016, August 24). *The truth about your favourite sugar alternatives.* Women's Health Magazine. https://www.womenshealthmag.com/uk/food/healthy-eating/a704690/best-sugar-alternatives-actually-healthy

Rita, P., & Datta, A. (2011). An updated overview on peppermint (Mentha piperita L.). *Int. Res. J. Pharm.* 2. 1-10. https://www.researchgate.net/publication/284341528_An_updated_overview_on_peppermint_Mentha_piperita_L

Ruhl, C. (2020, July 9). *Stages of sleep: REM and bon-REM sleep cycles.* Simply Psychology. https://www.simplypsychology.org/sleep-stages.html

Sánchez López de Nava, A., & Raja, A. (2020). *Physiology, metabolism.* PubMed. https://www.ncbi.nlm.nih.gov/books/NBK546690

7 ways to incorporate tea into your daily life. (2023, June 12). The Tea Shelf. https://www.theteashelf.com/blogs/news/7-ways-to-incorporate-tea-into-your-daily-life#:~:text=Refresh%20with%20a%20tea%20bath

Shah, S. A., et al. (2007). Evaluation of echinacea for the prevention and treatment of the common cold: a meta-analysis. *The Lancet. Infectious Diseases,* 7(7), 473–480. https://doi.org/10.1016/S1473-3099(07)70160-3

6 delicious anti-inflammatory teas. (2019, July 17). Healthline. https://www.healthline.com/nutrition/anti-inflammatory-tea

Skincare herbal teas - For drinking, toning and facial steams. (n.d.) Farm Soap. https://farmsoapco.com/skincare-herbal-teas

Streit, L. (2019, August 14). *The 9 best teas for digestion.* Healthline. https://www.healthline.com/nutrition/tea-for-digestion

Tea before bed and 5 other bedtime rituals for mindful sleeping. (n.d.). Plum Deluxe Tea. https://www.plumdeluxe.com/blogs/blog/tea-before-bed

Teas recipes. (n.d.). Rebecca's Herbal Apothecary. https://www.rebeccasherbs.com/pages/recipes-tea

Tea traditions, tea culture of the world, tea history. (n.d.).The Tea Spot. https://www.theteaspot.com/pages/tea-traditions

10 best teas for menopause hot flashes and other symptoms. (2018, February 21). Healthline. https://www.healthline.com/health/menopause/tea-for-menopause#fa-qs

10 proven ginseng tea benefits. (2022, July 27). Tea-and-Coffee. https://www.tea-and-coffee.com/blog/ginseng-benefits

12 best anti-inflammatory teas for pain relief. (2023, February 15). The Good Body. https://www.thegoodbody.com/best-teas-for-pain-reliefn

Volume of tea consumption worldwide from 2012 to 2025. (2023) Statista. https://www.statista.com/statistics/940102/global-tea-consumption/#:~:text=In%202022%2C%20global%20consumption%20of,7.4%20billion%20kilograms%20by%202025

What causes a person to develop allergies? (2018, September 21). Carolina Asthma & Allergy. https://www.carolinaasthma.com/blog/what-causes-a-person-to-develop-allergies

What is detoxification? Its types and benefits. (2023, March 21). Bansal Hospital Bhopal. https://bansalhospital.com/what-is-detoxification-its-types-and-benefits

Winchester, N. (2021). *Women's health outcomes: Is there a gender gap?* Lords Library. https://lordslibrary.parliament.uk/womens-health-outcomes-is-there-a-gender-gap

Yamprasert, R., et al.. (2020). Ginger extract versus Loratadine in the treatment of allergic rhinitis: a randomized controlled trial. *BMC Complementary Medicine and Therapies*, *20*(1). https://doi.org/10.1186/s12906-020-2875-z

Zelman, D. (2020). *What is inflammation?* WebMD. https://www.webmd.com/arthritis/about-inflammation

Made in the USA
Monee, IL
09 October 2024

67550484R00095